OTHER BOOKS BY THIS AUTHOR

The Republic of Texas

History of Texas

El Presidente; Life of Santa Anna

San Jacinto, the 16th Decisive Battle

The Lone Star State
A Textbook Taught in the Texas Schools

Remember Goliad

The Isle of Mal Hado
and Other Sketches

*Three Hundred and Fifty Years
of Texas History*

By CLARENCE WHARTON

THE ISLE OF MAL HADO
AND OTHER SKETCHES

DEDICATED TO

MRS. ADELE SPOONTS WHARTON

Library of Congress Catalog Card Number: 68-24648

PREFACE

These sketches which begin with the first white man to touch the soil of Texas, thrown ashore by a hurricane, and end with the passing of the red man from Texas three and one-half centuries later, give an accurate outline of the history of the largest State in the Union. It is the most dramatic of all our State histories, and involves the passing of nations and races. Texas is about to celebrate the first Centennial of the era of the Republic.

The flags of six nations have floated over Texas, and it has played an important part in the history of the western world. San Jacinto, fought twenty-one years after Waterloo, was the sixteenth decisive battle of the world. It wrought the independence of Texas and opened the way to the Pacific.

All the people who dwell in the one million square miles won at San Jacinto and in the Mexican War which followed might well be interested in the dramatic story of the Commonwealth of Texas.

C. R. WHARTON.

Bay Ridge, September 21, 1934.

TABLE OF CONTENTS

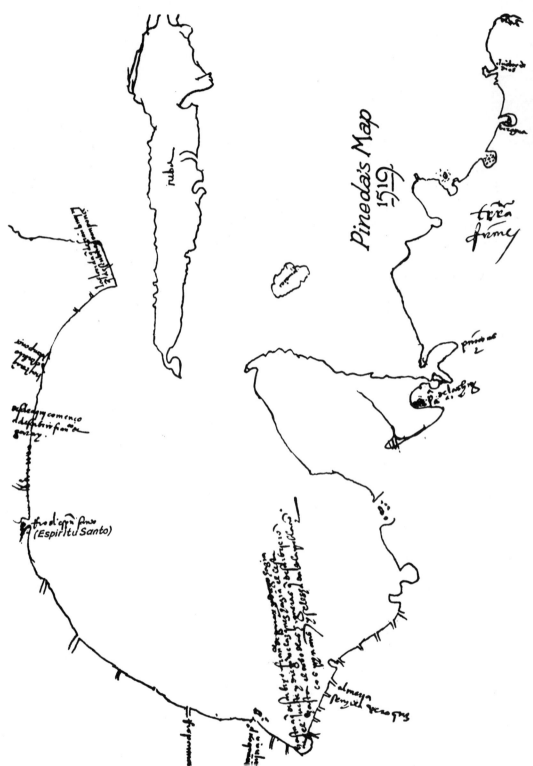

The first white man who saw the shores of Texas was one Alonso Alvarez de Pineda, who sailed from Jamaica in 1518, twenty years after Columbus' first voyage. Pineda skirted the north shore line of the Gulf from Florida to Tampico, and went home and made a map which to this day is known as Pineda's Map.

Pineda's Map
1519

rubn

tᵉa frmᵉ

pᵉᵈᵃˢ L

paᶜˡˢᵇᵍ

almayᵃ fᵉⁿᵧˢᵉˡ qᵉᵃᵒᵍᵗˢ

ſʳᵒᵈⁱᵉᵍᵃᵃ ſⁱⁿᵒ
(Espíritu Santo)

THE ISLE OF MAL HADO

The conquest of Mexico and Peru, about thirty years after Columbus discovered America, and the vast treasures of gold found there, threw Europe in general, and Spain in particular, into a wild fever of excitement.

Poor and ragged adventurers like Pizarro, lately a street gamin in Truxello, and Cortez, a small town lad who found his way to the New World at 19, became wealthy and famous. For their success they were accorded the high sounding name of "Conquerors." With the sword in one hand and the cross in the other they strode up and down the Americas, plundering, enslaving and murdering the natives. Pope Alexander the VI, of infamous memory, seeing that Spain would take the New World, hastened to make a grant of it to the King of Spain, who went by the high sounding title, "His Most Catholic Majesty."

These pious frauds were horrified to find the Indians making human sacrifices to their heathen gods. In order to put a stop to this awful practice, they introduced the "true" religion and backed it by fire and sword.

In the square across from where the priests of Montezuma tore the hearts from living victims on their bloody altars, the apostles of the Blessed Virgin built the chamber of horrors of the inquisition, where heretics were burned at the stake.

The first white men to set foot on our shores were the remnant of the ill-fated fleet of Narvaez, who landed on the Isle of Mal Hado in 1528.

One who does not understand these Spanish words might fancy that this is one of the enchanted islands that lie far away in some "Cinnamon Sea." But not so, it is a real island, and on its strand four hundred odd years ago the first white man walked the shores of Texas. If you will examine the coastal map of Galveston Bay and its environs and follow West Bay to San Luis Pass, you will see

The Savage Way. The Indians worshiped an unknown and terrible God with human sacrifice. This met the stern displeasure of the Christian Spaniards.

across the Pass a long strip of land which stretches down toward the
mouth of Oyster Creek some fifteen or twenty miles. It lies between
the Gulf and a shallow body of water called on the map Oyster Bay.
On the official Land Office map it is called Stephen F. Austin Peninsula, and joins the mainland a few miles east of the mouth of Oyster
Creek. In dry weather and low tides it is a peninsula. But when
storms blow and the tides are high and break over the low land at
the west end, it is an island. It presents a low marsh, miles of stub-
born salt grass, a treeless plain. This is the Spanish Island of Mal
Hado, which rendered in English means bad luck.

In the year of our Lord one thousand five hundred and twenty-
seven, when the Spanish gold hunters were abroad ransacking the
newly discovered Western World, a Spanish gentleman of high degree
named Panfileo de Narvaez, already famed as an explorer, set sail

The Christian Way. To teach the Indians the true religion, the Spaniards
smote them with fire and sword, and destroyed their temples.

[3]

from Spain with a commission from his Catholic Majesty, Charles V, to explore the north coast of the Gulf of Mexico. It was hoped that other gold-bearing tribes could be found here on the north rim of the Gulf like those so lately discovered and plundered in Mexico and Peru.

In due time the expedition reached the West Florida Coast, where it encountered a tropical hurricane, which destroyed the ships and cast the men ashore. The nearest European settlement on the Gulf shore was at Panuco, Tampico of our day, and the two hundred ship-wrecked sailors set themselves to the task of reaching Panuco, which they believed was not very far away.

They built rafts with immense logs, and with about fifty men huddled on each of these rude boats, took to the open sea. Soon separated by winds and waves, the water-logged fleet made its way up the coast, and on the 5th day of November, 1528, one of the rafts was

The first white men to set foot on our shores were the remnant of the ill-fated fleet of Narvaez which was destroyed by a tropical hurricane in 1528. De Vaca and his companions were thrown ashore from this fleet on the Isle of Mal Hado.

driven ashore on the west end of Mal Hado, and the very next day another crew was stranded on the other end of the island, though they had not seen or heard of each other for many days. About eighty Spaniards were thus thrust ashore, the first white men to touch Texas.

But these seafaring men were far from happy. Half starved, and most of them as naked as the day they were born, they were cast ashore in a November norther. De Narvaez and most of his officers had been long lost, and Cabeza de Vaca, the treasurer of the expedition, had assumed a kind of command of this miserable remnant. He directed Lope de Oviedo to climb a tree and take a look for Panuco. The island must have been higher then than today, for there is not now a tree on it save some scrubby salt cedar.

The island was inhabited by a tribe of Indians almost as naked as the Spaniards, who lived on a kind of root which they dug out of the shallow water and such fish as they could catch. Though the natives had never seen or heard of white men, they received these naked, miserable shipwrecks kindly, and shared with them their scanty fare.

During the winter 1528-29 about sixty of the Spaniards died of cholera, and the infection spread to the Indians, who had never known the disease before. They were so reduced by starvation that on one occasion survivors ate the flesh of their dead comrades. The Indians saw this and were so outraged that they were about to put the remnant to death. But through the intercession of de Vaca, who promised better conduct, they were spared for a worse fate.

Three hundred years later, when the first people from the States came to these shores, they accused the Krankaway Indians, who still lived along this coast, of cannibalism. If true, which may be doubted, they had acquired the habit from the white man, who taught the American Indian most of his vices.

During the year which followed their landing, most of them died, and several of the more hardy had gone on ahead in an effort to reach Panuco, which they hoped was not far down the coast.

De Vaca was for a long time ill with fever, and could not follow, and Oveida settled down on Mal Hado, and would not leave it. As time wore on, the Indians grew tired of their burdensome guests, and

[5]

de Vaca was put to hard work digging roots and hunting fish. And so the Conquistadore who had crossed the ocean to find gold was put to the ignoble task of digging briar roots and oysters, working as a slave for the savage natives.

In the summer months, when the south winds blew, they fared fairly well, but when the winter northers and sleet and snow came, the naked Spaniard suffered pain almost to death. When the full summer moon lighted the beach the natives held wierd ceremonies, and would dance the night away, while the poor, half-starved Spaniards sat by and thought of the moonlit hills of home. To enliven the evenings, the Indians drank a brew made of Yupon leaves.

By midsummer of 1530 all the Spaniards were dead except a small party who had pushed on ahead seeking Panuco, and de Vaca and Ovieda. De Vaca spent most of these summer months inland along the valley of Oyster Creek, but Ovieda stuck to his island. De Vaca plead with him to join in a getaway from their savage masters, and Ovieda promised and delayed and promised again to go next season. All the while de Vaca would not leave him.

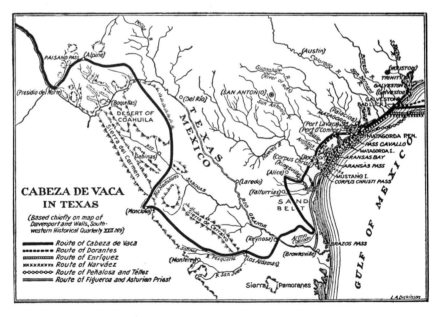

This map shows the wanderings of de Vaca into Texas at Mal Hado and across the Continent to the Gulf of California, 400 years ago.

In the late summer of 1532, nearly four years after they landed on the godforsaken island, they started west, Ovieda quarreling and urging that he be left alone to die on Mal Hado. They crossed Oyster Creek, the Brazos, the Bernard and Caney Creek, and took their way down Matagorda Peninsula to Pass Cavillo, which they crossed with much difficulty. Through this Pass 154 years later the ships of LaSalle sailed into the Bay Espiritu Santo, as the Spaniards called it. They were the next white men to come to these shores after the Spaniards passed in 1532. When de Vaca and Ovieda ferried over Pass Cavillo they heard that three of their comrades, Davantes, Castello and the negro, Stephen, were down the coast a day's journey. They had gone on nearly two years before. Here Ovieda rebelled and would go no further, and procured some Indians to row him back across the Pass. De Vaca stood on the far shore and watched his canoe disappear as he made his way across the Pass on his way back to Mal Hado. This is the last record of Lope de Ovieda four hundred years ago.

How de Vaca and his companions pushed on and on until they reached California is a familiar story. Joe K. Wells and Herbert Davenport have studied and mapped their footsteps with great accuracy.

Somewhere in the sand dunes of Mal Hado covered with the seadrift of the ages lie the bones of Ovieda. Perhaps on a pleasant summer day, or by the light of the harvest moon, you may sail through San Luis Pass or drive down the beach of Mal Hado. As you do you may recall as you look across the dreary waste that it is a Spanish graveyard, where the dust of eighty Spanish gold hunters lies beneath the sand hills or covered by the wild marsh grass. It is interesting as the landing place and the sepulcher of the first white men to visit these shores four hundred years ago.

LaSALLE AT THE MOUTH OF THE MISSISSIPPI

On April 9, 1682, LaSalle stood at the mouth of the river and claimed the lands reached by it and its tributaries for France. Mark Twain says of this this episode, "Then to the admiration of the savages, the Frenchmen set up a cross with the arms of France on it and took possession of the whole country for the king, the cool fashion of the time, while the priest piously consecrated the robbery with a hymn."

LaSALLE, THE FRENCHMAN

One hundred and fifty-four years had come and gone since de Vaca and his companions had plodded down Matagorda Peninsula and crossed Pass Cavillo, when one day in February, 1685, the great, great, great grandchildren of the Indians who had seen them pass, and only knew of the white man by the shadowy traditions of this event, which had been handed down through generations, saw the fleet of LaSalle floating through the same Pass into Matagorda Bay. A little more fortunate than Narvaez, the Frenchmen came to anchor in the bay, but a little less fortunate than de Vaca, he left his bones, along with those of his men, in the hostile land that stretched before him.

On the shores of Garcitas Creek they built houses, a fort, mounted cannon, and unfurled a flag which bore the emblems of Louis XIV, the first settlement made by white men in what is now Texas.

Much had happened in the outside world in this one hundred fifty years, but little on these shores. All the while Spain had claimed Texas, along with the whole earth. All the while Mexico and its outlying provinces, all called New Spain, was ruled by viceroys sent over from Spain, but they had not only neglected to visit Texas, but had not even named it. They vaguely referred to the unknown lands north of the Rio Grande as the New Phillipines, to distinguish them from the Phillipine Islands, though indeed there was little danger of confusing them.

Charles V was gone, and his European Empire had crumbled. Henry VIII and his wives and his red-headed daughter Elizabeth, the whole line of Stuart kings, Shakespeare and Bacon, had come and gone, and a Dutchman sat on the throne of England.

Englishmen were feebly planting colonies on the Atlantic Coast, and Frenchmen were paddling up and down the Mississippi.

Spain was about to have some real competition in North America. The high seas were full of roving robbers, and when LaSalle's

LaSALLE "CONFERS" WITH LOUIS XIV

LaSalle hurried home to tell the king about his great find, and after a time was permitted to so do, humbly kneeling. He desired to look up the rest of the world for his monarch, and, as Mark Twain puts it: "LaSalle sued for certain high privileges, which were graciously granted by Louis XIV, of inflated memory. Chief among them was the right to explore far and wide and build forts and stake out continents at his own expense and hand them over to the king."

fleet was passing through the Spanish Main on its way into the Gulf, one of his vessels was captured and its records fell into Spanish hands and were carried all the way down to Mexico and laid before

MURDER OF LaSALLE

In February, 1685, LaSalle entered Matagorda Bay and founded the first settlement by Europeans in Texas. He had intended to land at the mouth of the Mississippi, but was lost and never found himself. Two years later, still struggling to find the Mississippi River, he was assassinated by Duhaut, one of his men. This occurred on March 19, 1687, near the site of the present town of Navasota. LaSalle's nephew Father Anastatius, witnessed the murder.

the viceroy. This worthy was outraged at the thought that Frenchmen had dared to intrude into the territory of his Catholic Majesty. This insult to Spanish sovereignty could not go unmolested, and these impertinent foreigners must be found and expelled.

So they looked up in the ancient records the Map of Pineda, and the wanderings of de Vaca, to locate their beloved country which had been so ruthlessly violated by French intrusion. The Viceroy Cande de Parades sent post haste for the Governor of the Kingdom of New Leon, which was somewhere up towards the Rio Grande, and bade him find and expel the French. The Governor sent his Captain

THE ALAMO

The intrusions of the French into Texas aroused the Spaniards down in Mexico, who had paid no attention to Texas since the days of the gold hunters nearly 150 years before. They decided to build forts (presidios) and missions here to save the souls of the Indians. As early as 1690 they built some pine log missions in East Texas, which were soon abandoned. In 1716 they founded the Mission San Antonio de Valero (The Alamo) on the San Antonio River.

Alonso de Leon with a company of soldiers and a squad of priests with a writ of ouster. After three trials, and as many years, the Spaniards, in the springtime of 1689, found the deserted habitations of the French on Garcitas Creek, while all about lay their bleaching bones. So Captain de Leon went back and reported to the Governor, the Marquis of San Miguel de Aguyo, and the Marquis Governor reported to the viceroy, and the viceroy made a long report to the King, the old, dumb, decrepit, childless Charles II, who was too busy making his will bestowing the Kingdom of Spain to take much notice as to what happened on Matagorda Bay.

MISSION SAN JOSE

In 1720 Father Margil de Jesus founded the Mission San Jose on the San Antonio River, a few miles below the Alamo. It was the most splendid ever built in Texas, and was embellished by carvings done by Huica, a celebrated sculptor. About 60 years ago a cowboy rode by the abandoned mission and threw his lariat over the effigy of one of the saints at the portal and dragged it down.

THE SPANIARDS COME WITH SOLDIER AND PRIEST

The Captain de Leon had reported all quiet on Matagorda Bay, and all the French settlers gone, but the Spanish authorities feared another invasion of the French or English from across the Mississippi, and decided to occupy the New Phillipines and make it safe for Spain, even as they had done in Mexico. There they had built five thousand churches, missions, cathedral palaces, and overawed, murdered, enslaved and "made Christians" out of the Indians. So they planned to extend this same benign salvation to the Indians in Texas.

In the furtherance of this politic and religious purpose, they sent Captain de Leon for a fourth time, with soldiers, priests, people, cattle, horses, and sheep, to found missions and settlements, to save the souls of the Indians, and keep watch on the French.

They passed the site of LaSalle's fort, and good Father Manzanet set fire to the last log houses in what had been LaSalle's Fort Saint Louis. On they went across the Colorado, the Brazos, the Trinity, and into the deep pine woods of East Texas. There they found tribes of kindly, friendly Indians called Tejas, and from this came the name of Texas.

And when the good summertime of 1690 filled the land with leaf and bloom, and the corn was high and green, they halted on San Pedro Creek, near where it flows into the Neches, and built a chapel. And at the feast of Corpus Christi they dedicated it, and raised the standard of Spain bearing on one side the picture of Christ and on the other the Virgin of Guadalupe, and the notes of the great hymn of St. Ambrose rang through the tall pines of the Neches woods.

But they neither saw nor heard of any Frenchmen, and soon the soldiers and settlers wearied of this well doing, and abandoned the lonely little mission, buried the church bell, and went back to Mexico, leaving their cattle, from which the first wild herds sprung. A quarter of a century passed before they came again.

[14]

All the while the French were making headway along the Mississippi, or in Louisiana, as they called the country, and one day a French trader named St. Denis showed up on the Rio Grande with bales of goods which he was anxious to sell for Spanish gold.

This aroused the Spaniards, as they had been stirred by LaSalle thirty years before, and the good Marquis Governor Aguyo, who was yet a mighty man on these frontiers, came with more soldiers, and many more priests, to renew and carry on the politic and holy

FATHER MARGIL

Father Margil de Jesus has been called the father of Texas missions. Born in Spain, he came to Mexico in early life and devoted 45 years in an effort to make Christians out of the Indians. More than once he walked barefoot from the City of Mexico to East Texas. He was a saintly soul in a Godless age.

[15]

plan that had been abandoned a quarter of a century. Missions were founded in East Texas, from where they could watch the French traders, and along the San Antonio River. They went down to Matagorda Bay and dug in the foundations of LaSalle's fort and found a cannon, which may be seen this day in the courthouse at Goliad. On this sad site they founded the La Bahia Mission.

During all the 18th century these missions were maintained in a feeble way. But the Indians of Texas, as the country east of the Nueces was now called, were a more vigorous and wilder type than those who had been so thoroughly "civilized" and saved down in Mexico, and the missions were sad failures.

Centuries were plentiful with the Spaniards, and they proceeded with a pace which seemed to say that they had eternity at their disposal in which to reclaim Texas. About the middle of the 18th century, when the French and English were at war over their boundaries in North America, France had relinquished to Spain its claim to

MISSION CONCEPCION

The Mission Nuestra Senora de la Puressima Concepcion was established on the west bank of the San Antonio River in 1731. It is about half way between the Alamo and San Jose. These three still stand in a fair state of preservation, and were the most important of the San Antonio group. They were dedicated to a high ideal, and were a dismal failure.

the Mississippi Valley country, or Louisiana as it was called. This left Spain master of the larger part of North America.

The Apache was the lord of the western borders, the Comanche of the great central plains, and the Tejas tribes still planted and harvested their corn and pumpkins in East Texas.

SITE OF SAN SABA MISSION

In 1757 the Fathers founded a mission on the San Saba, far in the Apache Country, in the vain endeavor to salvage the soul of that soulless creature. The other Indians, chiefly the Comanches, who hated the Apache, gathered a thousand warriors who came down one morning in March and destroyed the mission, all to show their contempt for their ancient enemy, the Apache.

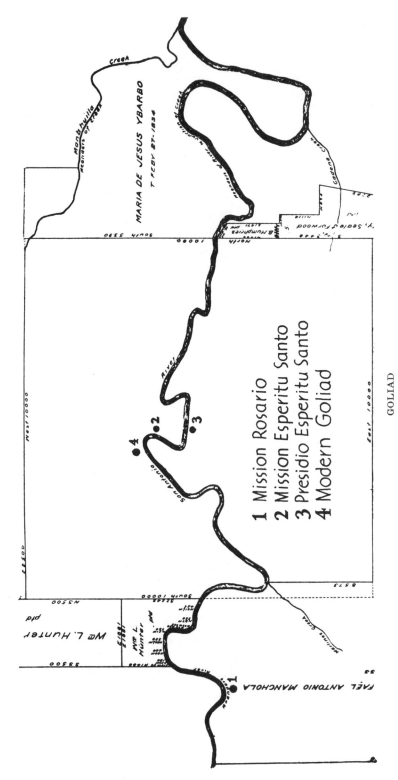

GOLIAD

One hundred miles below the San Antonio missions and on the same river, the Spaniards built a presidio and two missions. On the west bank on a hill they built a presidio enclosing about six acres, with a stone wall, and a mssion chapel. Up the river six miles was the Mission Rosario, and across the river a mile from the presidio, the Mission Esperitu Santo (Holy Spirit).

The Texas Chambers of Commerce and noonday luncheon clubs, had there been any, could not have reported much progress at the close of the 18th century. But things happened thick and fast in the early days of the 19th, as we shall see.

PRESIDIO CHAPEL GOLIAD

About forty years after LaSalle, the Spaniards built a mission and presidio on the site of his colony. When they dug for its foundations they found cannon which the Frenchmen had buried there. The mission and presidio were afterwards moved inland to Goliad, name and all. Here at this site the Goliad Massacre of Fannin and his men occurred in March, 1836. The old French cannon has recently been dug up at Goliad and may be seen there in the Court House.

THE BARON DE BASTROP
GOD-FATHER OF TEXAS

The last decade of the 18th century witnessed a series of events throughout the world which cast their shadows before. The French Revolution was at a high bloody tide. The Spanish throne was filled by the weakling Charles, who was ruled by a willful queen, who was ruled by an adventurer, Manuel Godoy, who was called the Prince of Peace, but who in fact was a sorry creature.

The United States had but recently become a nation, and its restless, roving population swarmed to the west in the vast regions beyond the Mississippi, which in name were Spanish lands. There was much talk that the Southwestern States might secede and form a new government.

The Mississippi River was under Spanish control, and the restrictions placed on its navigation caused an endless friction.

There was much talk that the people of these States would soon drive Spain out of North America. Louisiana, named by LaSalle, the Frenchman, more than a century before, was now a Spanish province, with a scant but preponderant French population. People from the States were coming in, settling here and there, trading with the Indians, trading with the French-Spanish population in defiance of the Spanish revenue laws.

Baron Corondolet, the Spanish Governor at New Orleans, fearing these Yankee intruders, afraid to try to keep them out, afraid to let them in, had a vacillating policy which varied all the way from strict exclusion to free admission. All the time he desired settlements which would develop the country provided these settlers would become loyal Spanish-Catholic subjects. But he, and especially his superior, the Spanish Intendant of the Provinces, was suspicious of everybody, and as cautious as possible about admitting newcomers.

Into this touchy situation came in 1796 two foreign adventurers whose names are to be forever linked with the history of the great

Southwest, the Baron de Bastrop, refugee from the French invasion of Holland, and Moses Austin, a Connecticut Yankee. That they came about the same time was a mere coincidence.

Austin, who was then thirty-one, was living at the little mountain town of Austinville, near Wythville, Virginia, where he had failed in a mining venture as well as several other varied ventures before it. He heard of the great country to the west, Louisiana, as it was called all the way to the Rocky Mountains, and decided to migrate. He had a family of small children; his son Stephen, born at Austinville, was five years old.

In December, 1796, he reached St. Louis, a trading post of two hundred houses, whose population was increasing at the rapid rate of one hundred per year. Twenty years later he told this story of his dramatic entrance into the Spanish Dominions:

When he came near St. Louis he deemed it wise to make an impressive appearance, and arranged a parade in which he rode at the head of his retinue, on his best horse, clothed in a long blue mantle lined with scarlet and embroidered with lace, followed by a cavalcade.

The Spanish commandant at the trading post, called the Governor, impressed with this show of pomp, received him as becoming his apparent rank and with proverbial Spanish hospitality, tendered him the country. He chose a location at St. Genieve, where there were lead mines, and got a grant of land, mines and all, and permission to bring in thirty families, whereupon he took the oath of allegiance to Spain, and became a Spanish subject. All this was in due time approved by Governor Corondolet down in New Orleans.

And while young Moses Austin was doing these things up the river, Felipe Enrique Neri, Baron de Bastrop, a broken soldier and a refugee, was approaching the same kind of a project down at New Orleans.

His proposal was to locate a colony upon the Ouichita River in what is now North Louisiana. Himself a refugee from the Fench Invasion, he planned to gather families of French Royalists who had fled to the United States to escape the terror of the Revolution.

His plan as unfolded to Corondolet and accepted was that each family was to have title to four hundred acres of land; that they would raise wheat, and he would build mills and have the monopoly on the sale of flour at New Orleans, Havana and other Spanish ports. He was to bring the families to New Madrid on the Mississippi, and the further expense of transporting them to the land was to be borne by the Royal Treasury. The government was to help sustain them for the first six months. He was to furnish rations and be reimbursed out of the "Royal Chest," a real and one-half for each ration, which was specified to consist of twenty-four ounces of bread, twelve ounces of fresh beef, or six of bacon, and a pinch of salt.

His proposal declared that the colonists would not use slave labor, and the cultivation of indigo, which was then carried on elsewhere in the South by this kind of labor, was to be prohibited. He saw visions of wheat fields and water power mills like those he had so long known in Western Europe.

Though it was generally known that wheat could not be grown in this region, this fact seems not to have been related to the Baron, and to have been overlooked by Corondolet. The grant was made embracing one hundred forty-four superficial leagues (French measurement) along the Bayous Saird and Barthelemy.

These things done, the Baron was off to the States to find his colonists. While he was under obligation to bring only Catholics, and, if possible, French Royalist refugees, he seems to have scoured the country and gotten them when and where he could, without particular reference either to nationality or religion.

In April, 1797, he was back at Natches, which was on the border between the Spanish country and the States, with sixty-four people, where he expected Corondolet to have a boat ready to transport them to his colony. He waited a month and no boat came, and he purchased a flat boat for six hundred dollars and put his sixty-four emigrants on it and drifted them down the river to the promised land. Later in the year thirty-five others joined him, making a total of ninety-nine, where he had hoped for five hundred families.

It was on this trip to the States that he met young Moses Austin at a wayside tavern, and they formed a dinner-table acquaintance and parted to meet again at Bexar twenty-three years later. These chance meetings are major events in the history of the great Southwest.

While the ninety-nine were raking the ground to plant wheat, Bastrop was busy about his mill project, and selected a site on the Bayou Bethelmy near its confluence with the Saird, and made a formal application to the Spanish Governor to confirm his choice. It would be necessary for him to dam the Saird, so he said, and he asked and got that privilege. It would also be necessary to keep the winding Bethelmy open all the way through the colony, he said, for this was the avenue through which wheat was to be transported to the mill and market, and if bridges were built across it boats could not pass. This winding stream twisted and turned nearly four hundred miles in going a headway of little more than thirty, and he asked for a definite grant of six toises above water level on each bank all the way, so he could control this sluggish stream. This was given, and strangely, it was held in after years that this strip six toises (about 36 feet) wide and four hundred miles long was all the land he got from the Spanish Government.

He was full of high hopes in these days, and made an estimate that when he had completed his venture, as he was now sure of doing, that he would have a profit of one million, four hundred thousand dollars, quite enough for him and his family, a fine fulfillment of his dreams. He set to work to build his mill, and there is much controversy as to whether he ever did so. At any rate, it is certain he never finished it. No wheat was ever grown on the lands, and no flour was ever made at the mill.

In 1798 Corondolet was no longer Governor, and his successors and the Intendant were not satisfied with the Baron's enterprise, and suspended his grant, and during the next several years he vainly strove by petition after petition, one of which reached the King of Spain, to have it reinstated, but with no success. During this time he occupied part of the land, farmed, traded with the Indians, and did his best to so establish himself that he could bring over his family from Holland.

He now conceived the idea that it was necessary to get some promoters from the States to aid him in his failing enterprise, and in 1804 he sold, if not all, most of his 144-league grant to Abraham Moorehouse and Charles Lynch, who afterwards claimed it.

Lynch was later identified with Aaron Burr when he undertook his wild scheme in 1807, and from this fact has come the repeated statement that Burr bought the Bastrop lands for colonization purposes. Many years later Stephen Girard, the Philadelphia millionaire, philanthropist, bought up the claims of Moorehouse and Lynch. When the good Girard came to die he made a will leaving large legacies including these lands to the Cities of Philadelphia and New Orleans, and many years later, long after the Baron, Moorehouse and Lynch were gone, these cities laid claim to the lands.

They brought a suit in the United States District Court at New Orleans to establish the Bastrop, Moorehouse, Lynch, Girard title, and the United States government, which had succeeded the Spanish and French sovereignty in Louisiana, resisted their claim. In 1847, after the old Baron had been twenty years in his grave, this case came on to be heard, and a jury was empaneled which, after hearing the evidence, the argument of counsel, and the charge of the court, retired to consider their verdict. The jury found that the Baron had fulfilled his contract, and upheld the title in the Cities of Philadelphia and New Orleans. But the Attorney-General appealed to the Supreme Court of the United States, and that august tribunal went deeply into the law and facts, and found that "de Bastrop" had not fulfilled his contract, and that the only land to which he ever took a good title was the strip six toises wide and four hundred miles long on each side of Bayou Bethelmy, which he had not sold to Moorehouse and Lynch. (See 11 Howard 609, 1850.)

But in tracing to its ultimate end the Bastrop grant, we have gone ahead of current events, which tell of the fall of both Spanish and French sovereignty in Louisiana, and drove the Baron westward into Texas. The Spanish sun was sinking fast in Louisiana when his grant was suspended in 1798. The Bourbon half-wit Charles wanted an Italian kingdom for his son-in-law, and in October, 1800, he traded all Louisiana to Napoleon, who had gathered up an assortment of kingdoms, for Etruria, in Northern Italy.

Then in quick succession came the sale of Louisiana to the United States, Austin, Bastrop and all, and though Austin cared little for the change, the Baron did not feel as though he was much better off, for Barons were not in high favor in the States in those days.

At that time Louisiana had a large number of refugees from everywhere. There were tories who had fled from the States at the close of the American Revolution; Royalists who had fled from France to escape the French Revolution; and others who had followed them on the advent of Napoleon, and yet others who had fled from far places for various reasons. Fugitives with broken fortunes and all kinds of schemes to repair them found little prospect among the gentry who were swarming in from the States on the heels of the American Army of Occupation.

The boundaries between Louisiana, as it had been purchased from France by the United States, and the Spanish possessions, to the west in Texas, were in dispute, and Wilkinson was rattling his sword on the border. It looked like war between the States and Spain. Many of these refugees of fallen greatness began to move westward.

Texas was theoretically Spanish, but in fact an unsettled wilderness, where the Indians held sway much as they had done when de Vaca landed at Mal Hado three hundred years before. There were only three Spanish settlements in all the country between the Sabine and the Rio Grande. Nacogdoches, with a population of seven hundred, Bahia (Goliad), six hundred, and Bexar (San Antonio), twenty-five hundred. There was a Spanish Governor at Bexar, and an Intendant over him down at Monterey.

There were the adventurers Bernado Despailler and Casa Calvo down at New Orleans, who, with many others, sought permission to move into Texas and bring with them dissatisfied persons who would prefer to live under Spanish sovereignty, and many petitions for permission to colonize these people in Texas were presented to the Governor at Bexar. The Spaniards were much concerned about Texas, which was the doorway through which the people from the States could come into Mexico and might take the rich mines of Chihuahua.

Forty years later when Manuel Godoy was an old fat exile in Paris, he told Dr. Ashbel Smith of Goose Creek, the Texas envoy to France, that King Charles at this critical juncture gave him Texas and he planned to make an empire out of it for his old age, but his plans like those of Despailler, Calvo and Bastrop went wrong.

[25]

In 1805 the Baron de Bastrop rode into Nacogdoches on his way to Bexar. He left ten years of failure behind him in Louisiana, but the hope that springs eternal lured him on. He would now go into Texas and Mexico to find the fortune and home for his family.

It was a three weeks horseback journey from Nacogdoches to Bexar, and the wayfarer must camp by the roadside, for he passed no human habitation all the way. Accompanied by three slaves and a French servant, down he went over the old Spanish Trail, which St. Denis had blazed a century before. He crossed the Colorado River at a place which thirty years later took his name (Bastrop), the only memorial to him in all Texas. He came as the agent of Casa Calvo to present a petition to colonize five hundred families

GENERAL JAMES WILKINSON

Commander of the United States Army in the days of Jefferson and Aaron Burr. He was rattling his sword on the border when Baron de Bastrop left Louisiana to take up his residence in Texas.

from Louisiana in Texas, and to present his own petition to be allowed to settle in Texas.

As he had done before, he evolved great plans and presented them in a petition which he filed with Cordero, the Spanish Governor at Bexar, in September, 1805. He proposed to bring in his colonists from Louisiana with a tribe of Choctaw Indians he had acquired there, and whom he recommended highly as brave warriors and skillful hunters. He asked permission to take wild horses off the Texas prairies to convey his colonists and Indians. Along with his petition he filed a manuscript telling Cordero and anyone else concerned what he thought of the Americans in Louisiana, whom he denounced as a daring, land-hungry, infamous breed, and disclosed their designs on Texas as he understood them.

All this sounded about right to Cordero and to Salcedo, the commandant down at Monterey, to whom the Baron's communications were sent by a special messenger, with the urgent recommendation that the Spanish forces on the Louisiana border be increased, and the borders guarded until help could be had from Spain.

Bastrop was granted permission to bring his Louisiana settlers and his Choctaws, and rode back in high spirits for them, but they would not come. He was not permitted to take any horses out of Texas, and was cautioned not to tell anyone in Louisiana of his permissive grant. Cordero and Salcedo were afraid these horses would fall into the hands of the land-hungry Americans, who would ride them back into Texas.

A year later the Baron went back to Bexar with another scheme. He wanted permission to open a system of trade with the Indians with a central warehouse at Bexar, and to trade Texas horses for goods in Louisiana, to be traded to the Indians. He was still unconvinced that the millions of wild horses on the Texas range should not be turned into commercial advantage. But this plan never got the slightest consideration.

As he went up and down the Camino Real he was impressed with the beautiful springs at what is now San Marcos, and sought permission to settle there, which was granted, but later withdrawn. So he settled down at Bexar, that squalid, far-away place with its mongrel population, where only the bare necessities of life were available in a most meager way.

When he first came in 1805, the Spanish officials welcomed him and the French emigres who would leave Louisiana to escape the American "Invasion." But after Napoleon tried to seize the Spanish throne, the French and many other foreigners were ordered out of the province, but the Baron was excepted from the order of expulsion. He now bought a house, not far from the Apache Crossing of the San Antonio River.

The deed to his house may be seen in the records at Bexar to this day. It recites that the property belonged to Don Francisco Roquier, who had given it to the Royal Treasury as security for an undertaking that he would return certain cattle, beasts of burden which he had taken out of the province with the object of bringing his family and goods. That having failed to return, the land was forfeited to the Royal Treasury.

It was sold to Don Felipe Neri Baron of Bastrop for $330, which he paid in silver Mexican coin. The property was situated on the river bank, had a frontage of 100 feet, "on which is located a rock house 20 varas long." The wanderer was now a householder and freeholder, and here he lived for many weary years.

His necessities made him resourceful, and he got together wagons, oxen, horses and mules and started a freight line to haul goods and supplies, principally for the army post at Bexar, from the interior of Mexico. It often happened in those years that all corn, and even fodder, consumed at Bexar, as well as everything else but meat, was brought all the way from Monterey.

These were turbulent years on the Bexar frontier. The Indians kept the population in eternal fear. The French menace loomed after Napoleon's invasion of Spain in 1808. The American menace was always present, and the Louisiana frontier was guarded with vigilance. A war for independence was going on in Mexico, and its echoes reached Texas. Boisterous bands of filibusters recruited in Louisiana and along the Texas border were coming into Texas and molesting the three little Spanish towns, Nacogdoches, La Bahia, and Bexar.

A young American lieutenant named Augustus MaGee, a graduate of West Point, who had been attached to the local garrison of United States soldiers at Natchitoches, aided by some refugee Mexican patriots, organized a mob of about four hundred men, which they called the Republican Army, and off it marched to the conquest of Texas.

After cleaning out Nacogdoches, General MaGee marched into La Bahia in November, 1812. There was not a soldier in sight. The Spanish government had kept a garrison here continuously since 1749 to ward off such an invasion, and the very first time in all these years that its services were required to repel a foreign foe the garrison was absent.

Salcedo was the Spanish Governor of Texas at this time, and he heard of the approach of the Republican Army, and had taken such forces as he could muster at Bexar and the entire military from La Bahia and gone down to the Guadalupe to ambush General MaGee.

But, like ships that pass in the night, these mighty motley armies missed each other, and when General Governor Salcedo returned to Bahia he found the invaders quartered in the town, squandering his military supplies, and a foreign flag floating from the church steeple.

There were stirring times at Bahia, the like of which had never been seen before. The Royal Army of more than a thousand men camped on the hills nearby and laid siege to the town. They had nine brass cannon, which would throw shot three miles. There were battles from day to day for more than four months, but the town and mission fortress held out. Sometimes the Royalist forces would enter the town, but the Republicans would rally and drive them back to the hills.

When provisions would be low a few venturesome filibusterers would slip through the lines and forage down towards the Guadalupe and come driving a herd of beeves which would be smuggled past the Royalist sentries. One day they were bringing in a white cow, and had all but gotten her safe within the fortress when she made a dash for freedom, the entire garrison after her. The Royalists were up and to her rescue and a battle raged on both sides of the river while the white cow made her escape over the hills.

[29]

General MaGee died on the night of February 1, 1813, of consumption, so they say, and one of his under-officers took command, and they drove the Royalist force back to Bexar.

There has always been much mystery about MaGee's conduct at La Bahia and his death at midnight, and many stories were told about the whole affair. One, that he tried to betray his men to the enemy, and agreed with the Royalist commander to surrender his whole army. Another, that his men deposed him and he committed suicide.

One of his compatriots in the enterprise was the celebrated Mexican Revolutionary leader, de Larra, who had joined him at Natchitoches and aided in organizing the expedition against Spanish authority. De Larra afterwards made a long report of the whole enterprise in which he says of MaGee: "He was a man of military genius, but a coward and a vile traitor," that he tried to betray de Larra to the enemy for fifteen thousand pesos and a position in the Royal Army. But he adds devoutly, "The Devine Omnipotence permitted this villain to fall sick and die as a result of some poison which he took to avoid being shot."

One would readily suspect that de Larra lent his aid to the "Devine Omnipotence" in this result, and that there was dark intrigue at the ancient presidio in those days.

After the death of MaGee the invaders marched on to Bexar and captured the town and put the chief defenders to death. In the high tide of their success, Arrodendo, with an army of two thousand loyal Royal soldiers, encountered them on the Medina near Bexar and routed them and chased the remnant out of Texas. Young Lieutenant Santa Anna was with Arrondendo on this memorable occasion.

All the while the Baron remained at Bexar, and his loyalty was never questioned. Nor was he pestered by the invaders while they occupied the town, many of whom from Louisiana had been well known to him during his residence there.

The war for Mexican independence kept on and on for many years, and was still going strong seven years later, when a young, ambitious physician of Natchitoches named James H. Long, encouraged by his pretty young wife, who was a niece of General Wilkinson, gave up his life of chills and fever to lead a Republican Army into Texas in aid of the Mexican patriots. He was burning with zeal to help the people in Texas overthrow Spanish rule, so they could enjoy the blessings of independence.

In those days the people of Nacogdoches, La Bahia and Bexar did not care a rap whether the King of Spain or some despot down in Mexico was their sovereign. They had no desire to be liberated by filibusterers from the States.

But this did not deter Dr. Long, who raised a rabble and marched to Nacogdoches, from where he issued decrees and proclamations while his turbulent bandit soldiers drove out the inhabitants and plundered the town. Two years later, when Stephen F. Austin first came to Texas, he found only twenty-two people living at Nacogdoches, and noted that it had been destroyed by the "Revolution."

Having thus conferred the blessings of independence on Nacogdoches, Liberator Long decided to extend the same favors to La Bahia and Bexar.

In the summer of 1821 he took up his headquarters at Bolivar's Point, across the Pass from Galveston Island, where the pirate La Fitte was then holding forth.

In September he left his wife and daughter and a few of his faithful followers at Bolivar and proceeded up the coast through Pass Cavillo, across which de Vaca had paddled, and where he had parted with Ovieda 286 years ago, and through which LaSalle's ships had floundered into the Bay 132 years before. Long landed and marched for the Royal fortress of La Bahia, which was the nearest place he could find to manifest his Republican wrath against kings in general and the Spanish monarch in particular.

Just at dawn they challenged the sentry and rushed the fort, which was soon taken without bloodshed. Don Francisco Garcia, who was in command, was easily converted to the patriot cause, and vowed himself ready to join the Republican Army of General Dr. Long. But secretly he managed to send an express to Bexar, and a few days later Captain Juan Perez of the loyal Royal presidio there hurried with a hundred men to the relief of La Bahia.

When he approached from the opposite side of the river, General Long went on the roof of Captain Garcia's house to get a better view of the enemy. While Long was surveying the situation, Garcia got hold of a gun and took a shot at him, which took off a lock of hair.

The battle raged for two days, when Captain Perez raised a flag of truce and invited a parley with General Long. At this interview he learned for the first time (so he said) that Long's men were Republicans and for the patriot cause. So was he (so he said), and why should they be fighting each other? They should join forces and march forthwith into Mexico. Long's men were induced to go with him back to Bexar to carry out their great scheme, and were made prisoners and sent into Mexico under guard.

This is the account of Long's quixotic fiasco which was given by his men, but a different version of it is found in the Spanish archives. After Long and Colonel Perez had gone, Don Tomas Buentello, the second Alcalde of La Bahia, having abundant leisure, felt called upon to make an official report of the affair to the Spanish Governor at Bexar, and he spared neither time nor detail. He advised His Excellency:

"The co-called General Long approached the town at break of day with much bustle and uproar, whereupon the first Alcalde directed me to remain and await events, while he went to gather up the scattered inhabitants. When I got onto the square Long and his fifty-one Americans and one Spaniard were taking possession of the artillery. When I addressed him through an interpreter he grasped my right hand, and said no harm would be done the people, and asked if independence had been sworn to. On my approbative answer he ordered one cannon to be fired twice. In so doing one gunner fell fainting and another had his face burned, and in the meantime a pistol hanging from a third man's belt went off and shot him through the leg, all of which seemed to make a sad impression on General Long. Then General Long asked me for a beef, and I could not refuse him, and directed Jose Trexo should furnish it. On the same day the first Alcalde called me and directed me to assemble the Ayuntamiento (town council) to call on Long, but that body passed a resolution that it would have nothing to do with that man, and all the members left town to await the troops from Bexar. The next day Long ordered me to supply him with corn, and when I

JANE H. LONG, THE MOTHER OF TEXAS

She was young and beautiful when she and her husband, Dr. James H. Long, landed at Bolivar, across the channel from Galveston, in 1819. They headed an expedition of adventurers called the Filibusterers who were bent on taking Texas from Spain. Left alone with her little daughter and a negro girl, she was rescued by Austin's first colonists in 1821. She was a niece of Gen. Wilkerson, and lived for fifty years at Richmond on the Brazos, where her descendants still live.

[33]

observed that the people were very poor he replied that he wanted it absolutely and I collected ten pecks."

In the same way Don Tomas continues his narrative, a kind of a daily diary, being careful to tell which citizen furnished each beef.

After Colonel Perez arrived from Bexar and went into camp across the river the second Alcalde became defiant, and refused to furnish Long beef and corn any longer.

"Whereupon he detailed seven of his men to catch some cows which were grazing on the edge of the town."

This brought on a general engagement in which Long and his army surrendered to Perez, "after which we all proceeded to the church and sang to Te Deum."

Whether we accept the version given by Long's men or the official report of the second Alcalde, the whole enterprise appears to have been a silly farce and Long a Don Quixote.

During the first twenty years of the century the people from the States had done little to ingratiate themselves with the Spanish authorities in Texas, and the recitals of these filibustering expeditions show how little they were welcome.

It has been nearly twenty-five years since the Baron first landed in Louisiana full of schemes for a fortune, all of which have failed; and since Moses Austin made his advent into upper Louisiana (Missouri) with schemes for a fortune, which have prospered little better. They have both taken the easy oath to the Spanish King, but he had traded them off, country and all, to Napoleon.

Austin, now fifty-three, was working away at his lead mine in St. Geniveve loaded with debt. His son Stephen was now twenty-seven. The lure of the West was still on him, and he decided to try another colonial venture. In December, 1820, he rode into Bexar accompanied by a negro servant and two traveling companions who had annexed themselves to him on the way. If the story of his dramatic entrance into St. Louis in 1797 can be believed, it had no repetition when tired and bedraggled he rode into Bexar twenty-three years later. He had no cavalcade, no blue mantle with purple lining bordered with lace.

He brought a carefully prepared petition to present to the Spanish

Governor for permission to settle three hundred families in Texas, and papers to show that he had been a good Spanish citizen. Antonio Martinez, the Governor, had been told by Joaquin Arrodendo, the commandant down at Monterey, to keep foreigners out, and above all, to watch those people from the States of the MaGee-Long variety who had caused so much trouble during the last few years. Martinez would not read his papers, and when the tired traveler tried to engage him in a general conversation, Don Antonio grew harsh and repeated his orders to get out.

The next morning as he was crossing the plaza between the Cabildo and the Cathedral, Austin saw the tall figure of the old Baron, whom he had met at a wayside tavern years before, when they were both planning their first colonial schemes in Louisiana. It had been a chance meeting in a tavern, and was now a chance meeting on the plaza, but it turned the tide of Texas history. Austin was ready to ride, and would have been gone in an hour.

For 25 years the old Baron had planned and failed, but he was not embittered, and in his closing years "had a humanitarian attitude towards all men."

He took Austin down to his little hut, and they huddled over his papers and talked over the colonial venture. The Baron went to the Governor with the assurance that Austin was a proper person, was too ill to travel just yet, and with the request that his petition be considered. They had seen Bexar stand still for many years while New Orleans and St. Louis and towns across the border were assuming proportions. These were the arguments for considering the petition of this trustworthy man who had been a Spanish subject, and who wanted to develop the country.

The kindly old man was heard with much respect by the quick-tempered Spaniard, and the town council was called in session to talk the matter over, with the result that the petition which yesterday Martinez would not read was received today and forwarded to Arrodendo with the recommendation that it be granted, which was done on January 17, 1821.

This was an incredibly quick transaction for Spanish officialdom, and the reversal of Martinez's expulsion order and the quick approval by Arrodendo were due entirely to the influence of Bastrop. From now until his death seven years later he was the patron saint of the colonies, and these years were the crowning achievement of his long life. Without him Moses Austin's grant would never have been made. Without him Stephen's success would have been doubtful. Texas and the colonies were the sole care of his remaining years. All the zeal he had manifested for his own ventures he had now for those of Austin.

Moses Austin went home to die and in the following August Stephen was in Bexar to take up his father's project. Here for the first time he met Bastrop, who devoted himself to Austin's plans.

On the 18th of August Austin filed in writing his plan for the loca-

Stephen F. Austin, the Father of Texas, was only 29 years old when he led the first colony of Americans into Texas in 1822 and settled 300 families under a grant from the Republic of Mexico, which had just become independent of Spain. The advent of Austin was the real beginning of Texas. The Spaniard had claimed the country for 300 years, but it was still wild and unsettled.

tion of his colonists and the distribution of land, and the document was translated and filed with the endorsement, "Baron de Bastrop." The proposal was that each settler receive a section, or 640 acres, 320 more for the wife, 160 additional for each child, and 50 acres for each slave.

This plan was approved by the Governor, and Austin was sent to explore the country down the coast along the Colorado and Brazos, and advertised this offer to proposed emigrants in the papers of the Southern States.

When he returned with his first colonists the following January, he called on Martinez for further instructions, and was told that

SANTA ANNA

When Mexico became independent in 1821, Antonio Lopez de Santa Anna became a leading figure in Mexican military and political life. He was a full-blood Spaniard, born at Jalapa, Mexico, in 1792, and for more than 40 years influenced and misguided the destinies of Mexico.

since Mexico had now become an independent nation, he should go down to the City of Mexico and get his father's grant confirmed.

Bastrop was little assistance to him in this important mission. He was never in the City of Mexico, as far as we know. But the old man was waiting for Austin on his return.

While Austin was in Mexico his first three hundred colonists were coming into Texas waiting for his return, selecting their lands for homesites, and impatient to have their titles.

SAM HOUSTON (1826)

Two years after Santa Anna was born at Jalapa, Sam Houston came into the world in Virginia. His widowed mother moved down into Tennessee, where Sam grew to manhood and became a soldier, congressman, governor of Tennessee, and then a voluntary exile among the Cherokees in Arkansas, where he became an Indian chief.

When he and Bastrop had conferred with Martinez in 1821 quantities of land to be measured in sections were agreed upon, and, as we have seen, headright for a married man was to be two sections, 1280 acres. But when Austin presented this plan to the new government down in Mexico, it would not hear to granting land in English sections. The labor, 177 acres, was the Spanish unit, and this was

Austin and Bastrop at the residence of Sylvanus Castleman on the Colorado, issuing land titles to the settlers, August, 1823.

the quantity an agriculturist should have. He was dismayed at this, and told them he had advertised the plan Martinez had approved, and his people had come in under this promise. So to please him and satisfy his people, they substituted the league for the section. The league, 4428 acres, was a Spanish unit, and each settler should have his labor and a league thrown in for pasturage.

Governor Martinez advised of his grant, and that he was on his way home, named the Baron de Bastrop, then second Alcalde of Bexar, as Commissioner to issue titles to the colonists, and in August, 1823, young Austin and the old Baron, riding from Bexar, reached the house of Sylvanus Castleman, on the Colorado River, where the people were assembled to receive them, and the business of issuing titles was begun.

Thomas M. Duke, one of these colonists, and afterwards Alcalde at San Felipe, tells about this occasion, and says that though Bastrop was then more than eighty years old, he was vigorous and alert, and told them how he had fought in the wars of Frederick the Great, and many interesting things he had seen and done in his eighty years.

From there they came on across the Brazos and down to Buffalo Bayou and the San Jacinto River, where numerous colonists had squatted, awaiting Austin's return. About two hundred titles were issued, all bearing the bold signature of Baron de Bastrop.

When they reached the settlement on the Bay, all the people were assembled at the house of William Scott on the land where the Goose Creek oil field is now located, and Austin made them an address explaining the colonization law. The day was marred by an ugly row between William Vince and Ezekiel Thomas, in which Thomas was knocked on the head with a hammer. All this unseemly conduct embarrassed Austin, and greatly offended the dignity of the Baron. But under the skillful treatment of Dr. Knuckles Ezekiel rallied.

They went on up the Brazos in search of the location for the site of the capital town, to be located. In the beautiful hill country in what is now Austin County, San Felipe de Austin was laid off and became the official headquarters of the colonies until the Revolution.

The next few years were full of care for Austin, who had all the

This freakish picture bearing the signature of Santa Anna was published in 1837 in Nile's "History of the Mexican Revolution." The signature seems genuine, but the picture looks little like others known to be authentic.

problems of the colonies and the colonists on his hands. In all these he had the aid of Bastrop, who saw in the growing settlements the fulfillment of his dream for a colony on the Ouchita, which had been shattered a quarter of a century before.

There are in existence a series of letters which passed between the young empressario and the old Baron, 1821-1827, which show their relations. In a letter to Austin of March, 1824, the Baron refers to "enemies of yours, whose conduct I have noted in sorrow, turbulent souls who are trying to harm you. But you should lay this aside and continue your undertaking. You have two friends—Saucedo (the Governor) and I." This letter, as most all his communications are addressed to Austin, "My dear friend and master." He had now put his entire effort, all his strength and influence, at the command of Austin.

A national government had been organized on the fall of the empire in 1823, and now state governments must be organized. Texas was without resources or population to become a State. All its people were in the three Spanish towns, Nacagdoches, La Bahia and Bexar, and in the new settlements which now embraced only about three hundred families. Texas had been annexed to Coahuila, and a Congress was about to meet down at Saltillo, and Texas should be represented.

In this letter of March 18th the Baron told Austin: "You will soon receive an order for an election of a representative to the provincial Congress. I believe the committee will elect me as the representative of the people on the Brazos and the Colorado. Many want me to go to the Congress, and if I had anything to live on I should accept it, as I am familiar with all this business."

He digresses from the matters of state to discuss some stolen horses which have been bought on the Colorado: "One belonging to Flores, and the other to the late Callontes, a bay horse they have on the Colorado. Saucedo has asked me to take special care of this business * * * send them here, not only the grayish ones and the sorrel colored, but all found in the brand I send you. Saucedo asks if the hat is made, he wants it English style. And two sticks of iron. If you do not sell the blue cloth, send me the piece with the vermillion that you have left, and make the price on it."

[42]

SAM HOUSTON (1834)

Foreseeing the destiny that lay before him, Chief Houston left the wigwam and became a citizen of Mexico in the Province of Texas, where he practiced law at Nacogdoches and San Augustine, 1834-1835.

Austin's contact with the market in New Orleans led the Governor, Bastrop and others in Bexar to make a kind of purchasing agent of him. In a postscript Bastrop tells him: "The business of slavery is before Congress. If there is some good tobacco send it to me if the price is not too high. It is for the Indians, and there is money in it."

On April 7th he writes:

"My dear friend and master,

"It may be they will elect me to the Congress, but I believe I must

GENERAL MIER Y. TERAN

Was a talented and educated Mexican statesman and general during the Texas Colonial Period, and devoted much of his time to Texas-Mexican relations, 1824-1832. Foreseeing the loss of Texas, and sad at the fate of his country, then dominated by Santa Anna, Teran slew himself in a fit of despondency in 1832.

decline as I am without means of subsistence. If I had means of living there I would accept with pleasure. I realize the necessity of sending someone who will take an interest in the Province (Texas), one who is acute and will not be dominated by delegates from other provinces, who can take advantage of the rivalries among them for our benefit. * * *

"It is very important that Texas have a Governor who is an in-

COL. ALMONTE, SON OF THE PATRIOT PRIEST MORELAS

This gallant Mexican was a son of the Patriot Priest Morelas. He was captured at San Jacinto and shared confinement with Santa Anna. He went to Washington with him when President Houston paroled them in November after San Jacinto. In later years he was one of those who invited Meximilian to Mexico, and when the Second Empire failed Almonte was driven into exile, where he spent his latter days.

structed man of moderation. If an unbalanced person is chosen we are lost. * * * Don't fail to send me the powder and tobacco for the Indians, blue cloth, vermillion and other things I have asked you for. There is no necessity for me to tell you what I want to do with these things. Don't forget the horse, send one with a good gait, for I need him badly."

One can see in these letters the pitiful poverty of the Baron and the depleted condition of his wardrode. He is old now, and needs a horse with a good gait, and craves blue and vermillion for raiment. Poor Austin is called on out of his scanty means to furnish all these things and more which are requested from time to time.

Then on May 10th he writes from Bexar:

"They are ringing the bell now for holy mass and coming from the church. I go to the meeting where they will elect a representative. When the election is over I shall finish my letter. * * * We have come out now, the election is over. * * * I was elected, but if you do not help me I cannot go. If you want me to travel send me *two* good saddle horses and a mule of burden, some money on account of my commission (for titles) * * * do not be short—you know the consequences. * * * If Goz has any more of the blue wool and cotton cloth send for a pair of trousers and a frock coat and some of whatever color for cape, some cotton or silk for jackets, a piece of linen for shirts, some neck handkerchiefs and some pairs of socks."

Poor, dear Austin must have groaned when he got this big order, and have felt he was a mere haberdasher for the Baron. Whether Austin was able to meet all these requirements, we do not know, but we do know that in the late summer, 1824, they had collected from the colonists $2800 fees for the nearly three hundred leagues of land titled, and that it took all the cash in the colony. That $1000 of this went to the treasury, and out of the balance the old Baron probably had the largest purse he had enjoyed in thirty years.

On the 22nd of September he wrote his "Esteemed friend and master" that he was off to Saltillo. "From Saltillo I shall write you. * * * It may be that I will ask you to send me a few head of cattle to kill in Bexar so that I may sustain myself. * * * I fear they will not give me anything in Saltillo. * * * I resent the misfortune I had in losing the two head of cattle I had with me, and I had to entertain John Austin like a Carthusian Monk on milk and vegetables. He will reach you as thin as a skeleton and as soon as he arrives you should kill a fat cow and feed him with restoratives. * * * Write me often, for you know the only consolation which remains between friends who are separated is in writing."

In this letter he tells he has sent a "document which in case of death I leave you and the Governor each one-third of my (unpaid) fees."

And so in the late summer of 1824 the old man is on his way to perform his last service to his "friend and master" and to Texas. We hope he had the two easy saddle horses and the mule of burden, the blue trousers and frock coat, and all the other articles which his need and his vanity craved, for he was on his last journey.

His demands on Austin did not cease when he reached Saltillo. In May, 1825, he wrote that he had negotiated to give the retired Captain Francisco Garcia fifty fanegas of corn (about 80 bushels) from the coming crop on the Brazos and Colorado. "Please give this gentleman said fifty measures at the place most convenient to you." Just what a retired Captain in Saltillo wanted with fifty measures of corn on the Brazos one cannot well imagine.

Again he wrote: "I have to pay Fernando Rodriguez 260 pesos. He has agreed with me to take it in merchandise that he may need in establishing the postoffice at San Felipe. Please give him this amount and charge to my account." On the bottom of this letter Austin, with his usual accuracy, took Fernando's receipt and filed it away.

In one of his last letters to Austin he says: "I have written you several times that I need five hundred pesos in order to leave here. I repeat this for the last time, with it well understood that what I ask for is mine. If it has not been collected it is that you obligated yourself to collect it. If it had not been with that understanding I should not have given the titles to anyone who had not paid me." The colonists were only required to pay a nominal fee of a few cents per acre for the leagues granted them to cover the expenses of the issuance of title papers, and the Baron's fees, and upon Austin's request credit had been extended to them with the result that he was being dunned in this strong language for their debts.

But regardless of his importunities, he rendered great service. Austin asked for a public expression on such topics as should be called to Bastrop's attention: Randal Jones of Fort Bend made some suggestions to Austin for needed legislation which he wanted forwarded to Bastrop. He wanted a law for the registration of marks and brands; one to prevent the killing of deer and wild horses for their skins, and another to prevent prairie fires.

At a meeting on the lower Brazos resolutions were adopted for Bastrop's consideration asking for a statute for jury trials and allowing the colonists to raise tobacco. He was also petitioned to procure a decree for the opening of a port at Galveston. The problem of law enforcement and protection against border bad men and the Indians were also thrust on him.

All these things and more had Bastrop's attention, and the journals of the Congress show that he worked with effect and had difficulties. He wrote Austin: "There is much opposition here to Texas. I must get the votes pledged before I present anything for consideration."

The first colonial grant to Austin was made by the National Congress and all other grants must come from the States. It was of great importance to get a colonization law at Saltillo which would enable Texas to become settled, and to this end, against prejudice, the Baron devoted himself. There were many would-be empresarios down at the little mountain capital, log-rolling for a liberal law. Among them Haden Edwards, who had long known Bastrop in Louisiana, Green De Witt, Robert Leftwich, and even old General James Wilkinson.

Bastrop's Colonization Code was all one could wish. Each empresario who would settle one hundred families would receive five leagues for his reward. The colonist would get a league and a labor, for which he would pay thirty pesos. A Mexican coming to Texas to live could get as much as eleven leagues. The colonist could select his own land and was exempt from all taxes for ten years.

Congressman Bastrop threw the door of Texas open to the world and bade all enter, select a league and labor of land for thirty dollars, tax free for ten years.

The chief question which engaged our representative during the entire first Congress was slavery in Texas. The first colonists had been permitted to bring their slaves, and others had done so without hindrance. The majority of the Coahuilan Congress were bitterly opposed to slavery, and not friendly to Texas. Its abolition would have been ruinous to the colonies at that time. The long debate resulted in a kind of compromise which made the children of slaves born in Texas free, and forbade the further importation of slaves after six months. A strict enforcement of this provision would have been disastrous, but it was never intended to be and was never strictly construed.

In one of his letters from Saltillo to Austin, Bastrop wrote discussing the prejudice against Texas: "It is necessary to be patient. After four or five years, when we have one hundred thousand people in Texas, we can give them the law as they now give it to us, or can separate from them. You may rest assured I have pulled every wire I can for Texas."

The same year Brown Austin, Stephen's brother, who was in Saltillo watching the Congress, wrote: "The old Baron has strove hard for us. I know not what would have been our fate but for him."

His last letters and his will are signed Phillip Enrique Neri. Under the Mexican Constitution of 1824 titles were abolished, and to show that he was a good Mexican citizen, he dropped forever his title Baron de Bastrop.

In addition to the extensive legislation for Texas which he procured to be enacted, he was active all the two years in urging upon the National Government such Texas relief measures as came under the dominion of national legislation. Chief among these was the tobacco question. The Federal Government had granted a monopoly on it to the province of Orizaba, and he worked hard to get permission for Texas planters to raise this product, but with no avail. The result was that an extensive and highly profitable tobacco smuggling trade sprang up between the colonists and Northern Mexico, where they would smuggle tobacco imported from the States.

All the while the Constitution of Coahuila and Texas was being drafted by a special committee, of which he was a member, and it was all but finished when Bastrop left the hall ill on January 3rd, and he never returned. On January 23rd he died at the house of Juan Antonio Padilla in Saltillo.

On the same day Juan Antonio presented himself to the First Mayor of the city and produced a formidable sealed document, "Which he verily believed was the will of Phillip Henri Neri." "In order that it may be known if he left arranged for his soul, I ask that you command that it be opened and reduced to public record." And the First Constitutional Mayor broke the seal, and perceiving it *was* a will, as Don Juan Antonio had gravely suspected, directed that the instrumental witnesses to the will be produced. Whereupon these four witnesses came before the Mayor, and having "made the sign of the Holy Cross," deposed that they had seen Phillip Henri Neri write and sign the instrument.

The depositions of all these having been reduced to record, the First Mayor then called the Doctor Cranel, who had also witnessed the instrument and the passing of the old Baron, and who added that he (the witness) was twenty-three years old and a citizen of the United States of the North.

All this seemed to fully justify the Mayor in reaching the conclusion that the document was the will of Phillip Henri Neri, and he boldly declared it so to be, and took off the last seals, and had it recorded in a vast volume, where it may be seen to this day.

It had been written on January 28th, after he had left the Congressional Hall for the last time, and reveals much of the long, lonely life of the testator. He tells: "I am Phillip Henri Neri, aged Baron of Bastrop. * * * I am ill, and confess all the dogmas of our Holy Roman Church * * * I was married churchly fashion with Georgaina Neyholt, Baronett of Nahylandsberger and have been a widower since 1811. * * *"

He gives the names of his four daughters and one son: "I do not know if they are married, for it has been many years since I have heard news from them."

"I declare that all my property in Holland was confiscated in

1795, but was restored to my wife in 1808." He then disposes of his property in America, which he lists in an ample inventory:

106,000 acres of land in Harrison County, Virginia.

100,000 acres of land in Ouichita, Louisiana.

A cattle ranch on the Guadalupe in Texas.

24 lots in Bexar next to the Apache Crossing.

A stone room on the corner of the park.

His lands were a myth. All his executors could find was the stone room on the corner which had been his humble abode for twenty years, and the Bexar lots near the Apache Crossing. Here he had lived his lonely life in Bexar without news from his family since 1811. Here he had entertained Moses Austin in December, 1820, when they planned the further appeal to Martinez, which resulted in the first colonial grant.

They buried the old man with due ceremony, dressed in a new suit of becoming black. A rascally Mexican, seeing him in this fine raiment, went to his grave that night and disinterred him and proceeded to disrobe his corpse. As he struggled with the huge frame of the dead man, the great arm fell on the little thief like a blow, and he fled in terror and told the priest what he had done, and how the Baron had smitten him, and the legend is that the thief died of fright that very night. At any rate, they went to the grave and found the body exposed, and reburied it and left the old man in the eternal sleep.

A week later Don Antonio Padillo wrote Austin, who was one of the executors in the will, that the Baron did not leave money to pay his funeral costs, "all of which with medicines and physician amount to 250 pesos, for which I have petitioned Congress for a loan which has not yet been granted. * * * All he left was some old clothes which I have given to the poor."

Thus passed in his old age and in a foreign land Phillip Enrique Neri, Baron of Bastrop, the true friend and faithful representative of Texas. He deserves to be enshrined among our truly great, and to be remembered down the ages. But for his intercession with Martinez in 1820, Moses Austin would have left Texas in an hour, and the first colony would not have been founded. But for his aid to Stephen during the first years, his close touch with the authorities at Bexar and Monterey, Stephen might have failed, as other empresarios did. But for his draftmanship of the Liberal Colonization Law of 1825 at Saltillo, further settlements would not have been made. In his very last days he saw the time when "we will have one hundred thousand people in Texas."

He saw the work of Stephen Austin a fulfillment of his own dreams. No fitter tribute to his memory can be found than the letter which Governor Martinez wrote to the Imperial Government in 1822, when all foreigners were under scrutiny: "Baron de Bastrop, who has been under the protection of the Spanish Government twenty-seven years, and in this province seventeen years, has maintained during all these years an irreproachable conduct. He has exhibited a humanitarian attitude towards all, and has performed interesting, loyal and confidential services for both Spain and Mexico, as the records will show."

This might well be the epitaph of this unusual man: Austin has been called the Father of Texas, and we may well call the Baron of Bastrop its Godfather.

THE REVOLUTION

It had to come. If the leaders in Mexico had not given a good cause for it, the thousands of newcomers who were pouring into Texas would have soon made or found an excuse for it. But it was not necessary for them to do so, for Santa Anna in his avarice and ambition furnished all the provocation. Bastrop's dream of one hundred thousand Texans had not yet been fulfilled, but there were more than twenty thousand in 1835.

The Mexican General Cos, with a substantial force at Bexar and a small garrison down at Goliad, stood on the frontier of Texas, ready to overawe the colonists.

About the time that hostilities began, Austin reached home after nearly eighteen months in a Mexican prison. There was a rally of Texas minute men to Gonzales, where Cos had threatened to come for a cannon which the colonists had long kept to scare off the Indians.

Austin, tired and pale, rode down to the Guadalupe and gave his sanction to the movement. He was the soul of conservatism, and had always been the friend of Mexico, and, until his last visit there and his cruel imprisonment, that nation had been bountiful with him. He was chosen Commander of the Patriot Army, and the cry was raised, "On to Bexar, and after Cos."

While they were executing this order, a convention of the colonies met up at San Felipe to consider the state of the nation, and back-woods statesmen swung into action.

There came to this convention, as a delegate from San Augustine, a powerful looking man in his forties, who had already had a career larger than falls to the lot of most men. Sam Houston had been a soldier under Jackson, now the President of the United States, and all the world knew that Jackson was his friend, and then, as now, the next friend of the President of the United States is esteemed for his good fortune.

Had Houston remained in Tennessee instead of resigning the governorship and exiling himself among the Indians, he would have been Jackson's successor, for the old warrior named his successor, and chose Van Buren because Houston had disqualified himself by his strange conduct. But what a tame career to have been merely the eighth President of the United States, compared with that which Houston led for the thirty years that lay before him now in Texas.

EDWARD BURLESON AT 30

Was chosen to command the Patriot Army at Bexar when Austin left to go as envoy to the States. When the city was taken he and Cos signed the Articles of Capitulation in a little stone house which still stands in San Antonio, and is called the Cos House. Burleson enlisted as a private in the San Jacinto campaign the following March, and fought as a Colonel in that battle. He was afterwards Vice-President of the Republic, and has left an illustrious family in Texas. His grandson, Albert Sidney Burleson, was Postmaster General of the United States in the Cabinet of President Wilson.

It is said that when Houston resigned the governorship of Tennessee and was on his way west and all Tennessee was wild with rumor, and his political enemies were filling the land with defamatory stories, General Jackson was seen sitting on the corner of a Nashville street with a rifle on his knee. Someone asked the grim old savage why this preparedness, and he laconically replied he was waiting for someone to come along who had anything to say against Sam Houston.

GENERAL MARTIN PERFECTO COS

Was commander of the Mexican garrison when the Revolution began in October, 1835. The Patriot Army of volunteers captured the city in December and Cos and his men were paroled. He broke his parol and came back with Santa Anna, who was his brother-in-law, in the invading army in 1836. He was captured near the Brazos two days after the Battle of San Jacinto, carrying a pitcher of water and an ear of corn.

[55]

During the years since Houston went into the forest, he had become a chief of the Cherokees, and the Indians in Texas just at this time held it in their power to wipe out the colonies while their available manpower was on the western frontier at war with the Mexicans.

In a quiet, dignified way, he towered among those who gathered for the consultation. He coveted a military command, and since the convention was about to send a committee to the States to seek aid, it was but natural that they would name the friend of President

BEN MILAM

Led the Patriot Army in the assault on San Antonio in December, 1835, and was killed. The following lines were published anonymously a few weeks later:

Oft shall the soldier think of thee
Thou dauntless leader of the brave,
Who on the heights of tyranny
Won freedom and a glorious grave.

And o'er thy tomb shall pilgrims weep,
And utter prayers in accents low,
That peaceful be the soldier's sleep
That conquered San Antonio.

Enshrined on honor's deathless scroll,
A nation's thanks shall be thy fame;
Long as her beauteous rivers roll
Shall freedom's votaries hymn thy name.

Jackson to high command. When he was chosen Commander in Chief, he might have gone at once to Bexar and assumed command of the Patriot Army, which was beseiging that place. Austin had left the army to go as envoy to the States, and Edward Burleson was in command. But Houston moved with caution, and allowed the Bexar campaign to work itself out. Ben Milam stepped in and took the glory of the Battle of Bexar, but Milam fell in the attack. Had he lived there is grave doubt whether Houston would have commanded at San Jacinto.

Bexar fell in December, Cos was paroled and went South. The Texans in the Patriot Army went to their homes. Only the adventurers lately from the States, who had joined the army for the love of a fight, stayed on. Some of them tarried about Bexar, but most of them went on down to Goliad, and towards the lower border, in hope of an expedition into Mexico.

Then there was the lull before the storm. It seemed simple enough to drive the Mexican Army out of Texas. No man is wise who despises and underrates his enemy.

But while there was a lull on the battlefront in the last days of the year, there was no dearth of strife up at San Felipe where the Revolutionary Government, called the General Council, held its continuous tumultuous sessions. No man among them disclosed any leadership, and the whole session is a record of petty intrigue which reflects no credit on those whose names are written there. They ousted Governor Smith and ignored General Houston, while they issued military commissions to Fannin, Frank Johnson, and others, giving them independent commands, with no army to command.

The stragglers, who, after the fall of Bexar in December, had gone down the Goliad way, were being exhorted by would-be leaders to follow them into Mexico. Those who remained at Bexar were waiting for something to turn up. And that something was no less than Antonio Lopez de Santa Anna, President-Dictator of Mexico, who with six thousand men was on his way north.

But there was another enemy of Texas at this hour more formidable and ferocious than the invading army of Santa Anna. The colonial settlements were all in Southern Texas, Bastrop was the extreme out-

WILLIAM H. WHARTON

While the Patriot Army was before San Antonio, the first revolutionary tribunal, called the Consultation, met at San Felipe, and one of its first acts was to name a commission to the United States. Austin, Dr. Archer, and William H. Wharton of Brazoria were named on this commission, and toured the United States, October, 1835, to May 1836, seeking aid for the Texans.

post. All of Texas north of the old Spanish Trail from Nacogdoches to Bexar was wild and full of Indians, who saw in the encroachment of the colonists their not-distant doom.

In East Texas were the Cherokees with five hundred or more warriors. There were Wacos, Lipans, Delawares, Kiowas, Osages, and many other small tribes north of the old trail, and to the north-west were the terrible Comanches with a thousand warriors. If

HENRY SMITH, THE FIRST AMERICAN GOVERNOR

The consultation of delegates from all the colonies, which met at San Felipe in October, 1834, set up a temporary government, but did not declare independence from Mexico. The hope was that there was a liberal element in Mexico which would join the Texans in resisting the tyranny of Santa Anna. Henry Smith of Brazoria was chosen Governor of the Council and James W. Robinson of Nacogdoches, Lieutenant Governor.

[59]

these Indians should go on the warpath, they would leave nothing for Santa Anna to do.

Fearing them, the San Felipe Council went on record for fair treatment for the Indians, and declared that the Cherokees should have their land, as we have ours. To keep them quiet, the Council sent General Houston to make treaties with them and give them these fair assurances. So, while the Council wrangled and would-be leaders dashed up and down the Brazos and advertised military ex-

DAVID CROCKETT

Next to Houston, was the best known man who participated with the Texans in the Revolution. He had long been a member of Congress from Tennessee, and when he was defeated in 1834, he said his constituents could go to hell, and he would go to Texas. He reached the Alamo only a few weeks before it fell. The story has long been told that after the fortress fell, Crockett had been captured and Castrillion would have spared his life, but Santa Anna would not let him do so.

cursions into Mexico by way of Matamoros, the old Cherokee Chief Sam Houston went into the woods and held a council with the Red Brother.

On the fair promises of the Council, endorsed by Chief Houston's personal assurances, the Indians remained quiet during the one hundred days while he faced about and drove out the Mexican invader. It would be a more pleasant task if the historian could tell that the Republic kept faith with the Indians, but it did not. And when the

LORENZO DeZAVALLA

Vice-President of the ad-interim government, 1836, signer of the Declaration of Independence, was a native of Madrid, Spain, but had long lived in Mexico, where he was prominent in public affairs. He was minister from Mexico to France when Santa Anna came into power and left Mexico to escape his wrath. He resided on his plantation on Buffalo Bayou, just across from the field of San Jacinto.

4th Congress repudiated the Cherokee treaty, Chief Houston, then a member of that body, bitterly denounced the bad faith of his people.

But the Mexican invasion could not be stopped by parleys, and on it came with the dispatch for which Santa Anna was famous. On Washington's birthday in 1836 he was on Military Plaza in Bexar, and five days later his aide, Don Jose Urrea, who had crossed the Rio Grande near Matamoros with a thousand men, was at San Patricio.

The General Council had about quarreled itself out of existence. About one hundred and fifty men, who had lingered about Bexar after the capture of the town in December, were garrisoned in the Alamo. The straggling troops, who had gone down the Goliad way, and some two hundred volunteers, who had come in by sea to Goliad, were scattered in small groups, easy prey for Don Jose. It looked like the hour of doom for poor Texas.

Under these doleful environments a Colonial Convention met at Washington on the Brazos on March 1, 1836, and a new assortment of backwoods statesmen swung into action. Whether it was a better body than the last one, or whether the dangers that pressed kept this gathering engrossed and gave no time for petty quarrels might be debated. At any rate, this last of the Colonial Conventions got down to business, wrote and adopted a declaration of independence; wrote, debated and adopted a Constitution; chose a President ad interim, elected General Houston Commander in Chief, all in the space of seventeen days, and got out of town just in time to escape the Mexican Army.

The little garrison at the Alamo calmly waited the annihilation which was in store for it. Col. Travis, who was in command, had no notion to retreat or surernder. He seemed to crave martyrdom and immortality, both of which he got. For more than two weeks they held the invading army in check, until on the early morning of March 6 at dawn the Mexicans carried the fortress by storm and the last of the defenders were slain.

Gen. Santa Anna rested a few days after this victory, sent one division on east, dispatched five hundred men to join Urrea, who was now at Goliad. He thought the rebellion squelched, and contemplated returning home, but Colonel Almonte urged him to see the finish of what he had so well begun, and he prepared to go on east.

In the meantime Don Jose Urrea had fallen on the several small detachments of scattered troops down his way and had killed, or captured and then killed them all.

On the morning of March 6, about the hour the Alamo fell, Major General Sam Houston, just re-elected Commander in Chief of the Armies of the Republic, rode out from Washington on the Brazos

MRS. LORENZO DeZAVALLA

Mrs. Lorenzo DeZavalla was an American woman of culture and charm. She had married DeZavalla while he was connected with the Mexican Legation at Washington. It was at their home, just across from the battlefield, that the wounded soldiers were treated. Most of the 21 wounded Texans died for want of skillful medical attention.

[63]

for the seat of war accompanied by two men, George W. Hockley and Richardson Scurry. Five days later these three horsemen rode into Gonzales sixty miles from San Antonio, where they found about three hundred volunteers, and heard the news of the fall of the Alamo and the approach of Santa Anna's Army.

At this news the Patriot Army beat a rapid retreat. They threw their only cannon into the river, burnt up all their supplies, except such as they could carry without hindering the march, put their war

CAPTAIN JESSE BILLINGSLY
Who led the Bastrop Volunteers, the first Company to Reach Gonzales.

Captain Jesse Billingsly commanding volunteers from Bastrop was the first to reach the rendezvous at Gonzales, and was there waiting when Gen. Houston and his escort arrived on March 11th, where he was met with the news of the fall of the Alamo. Billingsly and the Bastrop men retreated with Houston, and were in the Battle of San Jacinto 40 days later.

[61]

material on a single wagon, and in the glare of burning houses were off in the night to the Colorado River, sixty miles away, which they crossed and made a first stop.

Various companies of volunteers all the way from San Augustine to Brazoria joined the army on the Colorado and swelled its rolls to nearly 1400 men. An advance division of the Mexican Army, under Sesma, closely followed, camped just across the river, and

COLONEL SIDNEY SHERMAN

Organized a company of Kentuckians which took passage on an Ohio River steam-boat at Cincinnati in a violent snow storm on the last day of the year 1835. They came down the Ohio and the Mississippi, thence up Red River to Natchitoches, and marched on foot all the way to Gonzales, where they waited for General Houston. When the army was organized Sherman was chosen a Colonel, and as such fought at San Jacinto.

[65]

Santa Anna was on his way. It looked as if this were the time and place for the last stand of the Texans.

Just at this time a courier came with the news of the capture and massacre of Fannin's men at Goliad, and that Urrea was on his way to the lower Colorado. With the same dispatch that they had left Gonzales two weeks before, when the news of the Alamo struck terror to their hearts, the Patriot Army was off to the Brazos forty miles away.

All Texas was on the run, every family east of the Nueces which could get away was on the way to the Louisiana border, and those who could not make this long trek had taken to the woods. The roads were full of fugitives, and the river crossings were congested by thousands clamoring for ferryage. Children were born and old and decrepit persons died on the way. Measles broke out in the army and among the fugitives. Parents stopped an hour to bury their dead children, and hurried on. All men feared the fate that had befallen those at the Alamo and Goliad.

Houston reached San Felipe on the Brazos on March 28, camped there over night, and then for some strange reason marched up the west bank of the river thirty miles and camped in the woods. Mosley Baker's company refused to follow further, burned San Felipe and crossed over the river there.

Santa Anna left San Antonio on the last day of March, overtook Sesma's division on the Colorado on the 5th, passed it with orders for it to follow, and rode into San Felipe on April 7. The April rains had made the bottoms impassable, the river was swollen, and he could not cross, and he detoured by the Bernard and reached the Brazos at Richmond. Sesma and Filisola with 2000 men were following the fast-riding Dictator.

Up in the Brazos bottom, across from Groce's lower plantation, the Patriot Army shivered in the cold April rain. The nearly 1400 men who marched from the Colorado had dwindled to fewer than 1000. Low and dispirited, they muttered and threatened to remove Houston, and it was rumored that someone was going to drum up a mass meeting to elect a new Commander. Houston, silent and grim, kept his own counsel and posted notices on the trees throughout the camp that the first man trying these tactics would be shot.

When the convention adjourned at Washington on the 17th of March it had chosen David G. Burnet President Ad Interim, and he had chosen a cabinet, and they had hurried to Harrisburg on Buffalo Bayou, where they stopped thirty miles from the Brazos to

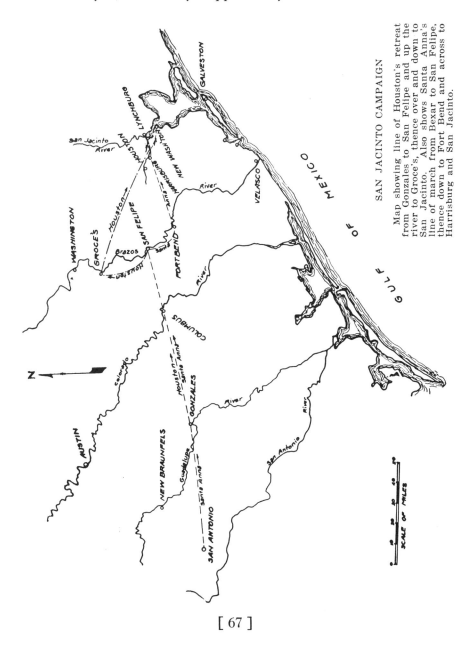

SAN JACINTO CAMPAIGN

Map showing line of Houston's retreat from Gonzales to San Felipe and up the river to Groce's, thence over and down to San Jacinto. Also shows Santa Anna's line of march from Bexar to San Felipe, thence down to Fort Bend and across to Harrisburg and San Jacinto.

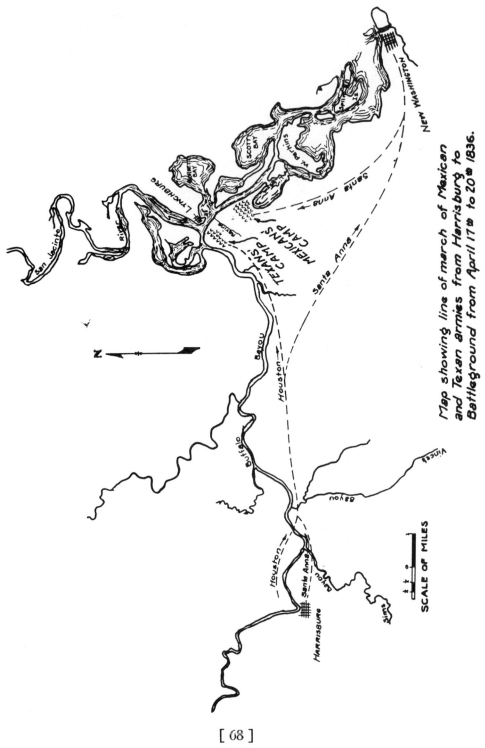

Map showing line of march of Mexican and Texan armies from Harrisburg to Battleground from April 17th to 20th 1836.

await results. Rusk, the Secretary of War, was sent back to meet Houston's retreating army with executive orders for it to stop and fight.

April 14th was a beautiful day in spring, radiant with warm sunshine, after the cold rain of the week before, in which the little brown soldiers from the tropics shivered and shook. On this day Santa Anna crossed the Brazos and was off to Harrisburg. He did not know where Houston was, nor his plans.

In fact, the Texas Commander did not know his own plans. He wanted to cross the Brazos and continue his retreat into the Red Lands, where he hoped for reinforcements, and to get as near the Louisiana border as possible. If he could lure the Mexicans that far, he might get them so near General Gaines' command at Fort Jessup on the Sabine that in some way he would involve them with these soldiers of the United States who were craving an excuse to get into the fray. Old General Gaines had not fared well in the recent Florida campaign, and would have given his immortal soul for a chance to get into this spectacular war.

Did Houston have some understanding with Jackson for help? All through the previous summer and autumn soldiers had been recruited in the States and marched off in military formation for Texas without serious hindrance by the officers of the United States, and in defiance of the neutrality laws. At this very hour Austin, Wharton and Archer, agents for Texas, were touring the States pleading for help for Texas, and were everywhere received with enthusiasm. The world will always believe that Houston's anxiety to lead the invading Mexican Army to the Louisiana border was a part of a plan.

Twenty months before President Jackson was spending the summer down at the Hermitage at Nashville, and while there he had long conferences with his close friend William H. Gwin, formerly of Tennessee, but now his United States marshal of Mississippi. Forthwith Marshal Gwin repaired to Nacogdoches, Texas, and had long conferences with Houston and Rusk, lately from the States. While there, Gwin bought some large tracts of Texas land for himself and certain associates, and went back to the Hermitage for another talk with the President.

What was discussed at these whispered conferences at the Hermitage and Nacogdoches one hundred years ago, shrouded by the veil
of secrecy and the mantle of years, the world will never know.   But

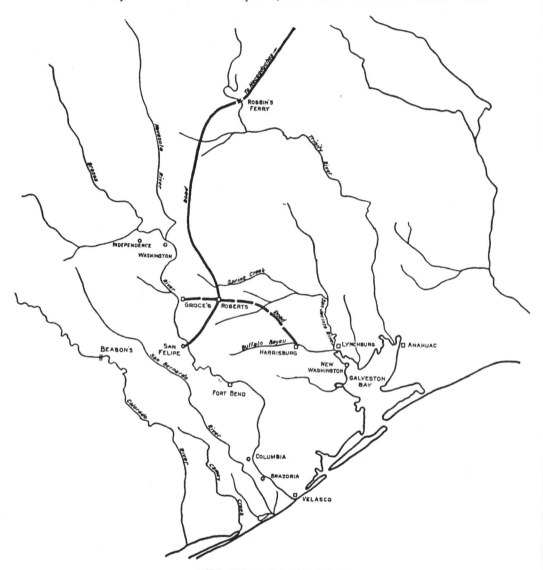

THE FORKS OF THE ROAD

This map shows the famous cross-roads at Roberts,' near Spring Creek, in Harris County, where
Houston's army coming down from Groce's on April 17, turned to the right to Harrisburg and San
Jacinto instead of retreating further into East Texas.   Roads of Destiny: If they had gone on into
East Texas, as first planned, would Santa Anna have consolidated his army and overwhelmed them?

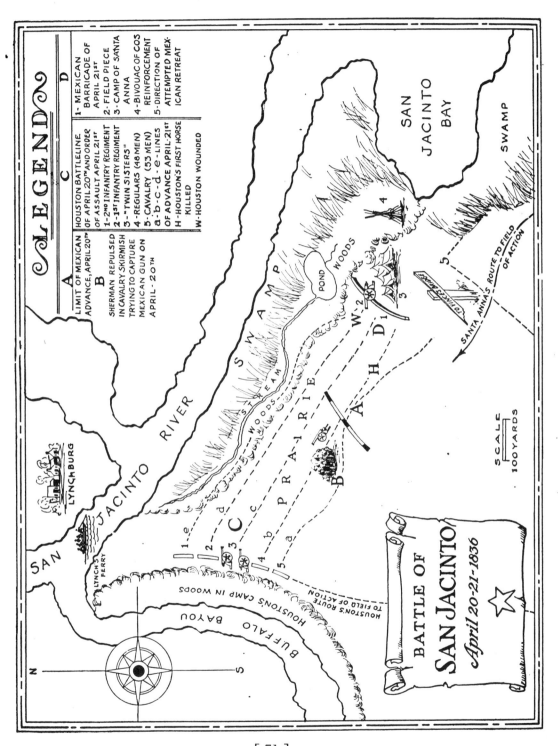

LEGEND

A
LIMIT OF MEXICAN ADVANCE, APRIL 20TH

B
SHERMAN REPULSED IN CAVALRY SKIRMISH TRYING TO CAPTURE MEXICAN GUN ON APRIL-20TH

C
HOUSTON BATTLE LINE OF APRIL 20TH AND ORDER OF ASSAULT APRIL 21ST
1 - 2ND INFANTRY REGIMENT
2 - 1ST INFANTRY REGIMENT
3 - "TWIN SISTERS"
4 - REGULARS (48 MEN)
5 - CAVALRY (53 MEN)
a-b-c-d-e-LINES OF ADVANCE APRIL 21ST
H - HOUSTON'S FIRST HORSE KILLED
W - HOUSTON WOUNDED

D
1 - MEXICAN BARRICADE OF APRIL 21ST
2 - FIELD PIECE
3 - CAMP OF SANTA ANNA
4 - BIVOUAC OF COS REINFORCEMENT
5 - DIRECTION OF ATTEMPTED MEXICAN RETREAT

SAN JACINTO BAY

SWAMP

SWAMP

SAN JACINTO RIVER

LYNCHBURG

SAN JACINTO

LYNCH'S FERRY

POND

WOODS

STREAM

WOODS

PRAIRIE

SANTA ANNA'S ROUTE TO FIELD OF ACTION

HOUSTON'S CAMP IN WOODS

HOUSTON'S ROUTE TO FIELD OF ACTION

BUFFALO BAYOU

N

S

SCALE
100 YARDS

BATTLE OF
SAN JACINTO
April 20-21-1836

[71]

this we do know: Jackson wanted Texas and California, and so did Gwin, who sixteen years after was a first United States Senator from the Golden State.

But Houston's Army was tired of retreat, and clamored for a fight, and Secretary of War Rusk was now in camp with orders from the fugitive President Burnet to retreat no further.

The steamboat Yellow Stone was in the river at Groce's, and at the same hour that Santa Anna crossed the river at Fort Bend, the Texans crossed on the Yellow Stone sixty miles above, neither knowing the movements of the other. And while the Mexican Commander dashed off through the plantations to Harrisburg after Burnet and his cabinet, the Texans plodded across the wet prairie along the muddy trail which led towards Robbins Ferry on the Trinity, and on to the Red Lands and the Sabine.

Three days later they were at the forks of the road, the left going east to Robbins Ferry on the Trinity, the right to Harrisburg. Before reaching there, Houston had surrendered his convictions to Rusk's entreaties, and had decided to take the road to Harrisburg, but had not announced his decision. Just here a colored boy came riding from the south with news that Santa Anna was at Harrisburg. This was the first information as to his whereabouts since he left San Felipe a week ago. The die was cast, the big drum beat, and the bugle sounded the forward march. Capt. Calder's Brazoria troops led the way with a shout. Houston sat grim and silent on his horse and watched his thousand men file down the Harrisburg Road, and bidding farewell to all other plans, was off for Santa Anna.

Just then Three-Legged Willie came galloping across the prairie from towards Robbins Ferry wearing his coonskin cap with coon tails hanging down his shoulders. There was a whispered conference, and plans for halting recruits at Robbins Ferry were abandoned.

The forty days compaign was about over. San Jacinto was but four days away. Those who question Houston's judgment or his courage are wrong. He knew no fear. He had seen the rash bravery of Travis and the foolhardiness of Fannin sweep away as many men as he now commanded. Six thousand victorious troops were after him. All Texas was abandoned and desolate. Thousands of Indian

JOHN AUSTIN WHARTON
"The keenest blade at San Jacinto."

John Austin Wharton who formed the battle line at San Jacinto and gave the battle its name. When he died in 1838 he was a member of Congress of the Republic, and his funeral oration was delivered by Ex-President Burnet, who opened his address with the famous sentence: "Comrades, the keenest blade of San Jacinto lies broken before you."

[73]

warriors watched from across the northern frontier and waited only for an opportunity to wipe out the intruders into their hunting grounds. A false step and all was lost.

For El Presidente, this dash to Harrisburg and down the Bayou was a joy ride. A long trained soldier, a fatalist, life to him was an avowed game of chance, and when he camped at Morgans Point on the night of the 19th, he looked out across the sea whose tide washed the far shores of his empire, the third largest in territorial limits of

HENRY WAX KARNES
(From sketch by McArdle)

Soldier at San Jacinto, was then 24 years old, and won distinction. The average age of the Texans in that battle was about 24, many of the men were younger. More than half of them had come to Texas within the last few months to take part in the war. Karnes was an overseer on the Groce plantation when the war began. He died in 1840 from wounds received in an Indian fight.

the nations of the earth.   In battle formation, marching to the sounds of martial music, whose strains had inspired his Spanish ancestors for centuries, he doubled back to the Lynchburg Ferry on the morning of the 20th.   He had now heard, for the first time since he left San Felipe, where Houston was.

Just before the sounds of the Mexican music, borne on the soft south wind, were audible to the Texans, now camped a mile from the Lynchburg Ferry, a colored boy named Turner, one of old Mor-

THE SHERMAN FLAG
*Borne by Jas. A. Sylvester, who was one of the Captors
of Santa Anna the next day.*

Carried by Sherman's company of Kentuckians. His sweetheart's glove was tied to the flag staff. The flag has been preserved and is now (1934) hanging in the House of Representatives at Austin, just behind the speaker's stand. The company carrying this flag was on the extreme left in the battle line.

gan's slaves, came riding from the south with the news that Santa Anna was coming.

The armies camped that night a mile apart, and through the twilight and at dawn there was a desultory artillery duel. The Texans had two small cannon and the Mexicans one, but the cannonading was as harmless as the music.

The armies were not far from the same size, but Santa Anna did not believe that the Texans would fight. He thought they were trying to get to the ferry and across the Bayou and the San Jacinto River. On the afternoon of April 21st, tired and oppressed with the heat of the April day, so he says, he had lain down in the shade of the oaks for his siesta, as Mexican gentlemen had ever done, and "when I was awakened they were rudely threatening my person with their guns."

While the Commander slept, the lesser officers did likewise, and the soldiers were at ease. They did not think the Texans would fight, and kept no sentinels posted.

At 4 p. m. General Houston gave the order to Colonel Wharton to form a battle line, and at 4:15 p. m. it was off across the prairie, a single line of a thousand yards of infantry, a thousand men shoulder to shoulder. On the far left was Sidney Sherman. In the center rode Sam Houston. On the far right Lamar with 64 mounted men.

The average age of the Texas soldier was well under thirty, many were boys of seventeen. None of them had ever seen a battle, and their Commander had only fought in one battle, when he was wounded at Horse Shoe Bend, twenty-odd years before. A single volley well directed at this thin line of boy soldiers as it crossed the plain and up the hill would have broken it in a hundred places. But the volley was never fired, the surprise was as complete as if executed at moonless midnight.

Dapper Colonel Delgado heard a Mexican bugler sound the warning, and stepped up on the cannon frame and looked down the hill. "I saw the Texans coming in a line, wide extended, and in the center a flag." There was no battle, but a rout and a slaughter, and in the midst of it Deaf Smith came dashing on a foaming horse, brandishing an axe, and yelling, "I have destroyed Vince bridge."

The Mexican Army was killed or captured. The Texans lost about twenty men. Sundown and twilight brought a lull, and the full moon rose over the landscape. In its soft light many a gallant soldier saw the last glimpse of this cruel world, and down in the woodlands wolves, scenting blood, filled the night with hideous howls.

All through the night couriers were leaving the Texas camp to overtake the fugitive Texans of the "Run Away Scrape," as they always called their flight, and tell them the news. One of these frontier riders dashed into Gen. Gaines' camp on the Neches with a message written on a sheet of waste paper, in lead pencil, telling in one

DEATH OF CASTRILLION
(From painting by McArdle.)

General Castrillion was a Spaniard. He led the assault at the Alamo and was generous and brave. His remains were interred at the DeZavalla burial ground across the bayou from the battlefield. In 1928 I had them disinterred and taken to the battleground for reinterment, but due to a misunderstanding among the DeZavalla descendants, took them back to his old grave, where they will remain to the end of time.

[77]

sentence of the great victory. It was addressed to no one, and ended with, "Let the people come home and plant corn," and signed Sam Houston. General Gaines called Lieutenant Ethan Allen Hitchcock, a grandson of Ethan Allen of Ticonderoga, and bade him go forthwith to Washington and deliver it to President Jackson.

Three weeks later the messenger bearing the most momentous news since the Battle of Waterloo handed it to the old warrior President at the White House, and the next day San Jacinto was news in the Washington papers. The Lieutenant says the old man was wild with

DR. LABADIE

Was a private in Capt. Logan's Liberty Volunteers; after the war he was a bitter partisan against General Houston, and wrote articles denouncing him. Said Houston intended to take the Robbins Ferry Road at Roberts, but his men forced him to go to Harrisburg. After the war he conducted a drug store at Galveston.

delight, and read and re-read the note, exclaiming, "That's Sam Houston's writing, I know it well." It may be this was the fulfillment of the plans of Jackson, Houston, Rusk and William M. Gwin.

The tired mother who, far from her cabin home, nursed her sick babe that night in a refugee camp on the Trinity or the Sabine, and who feverishly prayed for deliverance, felt her prayers answered when the next day a horseman dashed by broadcasting the victory.

The avenging angel who smote the army of Sennecherib did not do a more thorough job. The forty days were over now, and Texas

DR. WILLIAM MOTTLEY \

Delegate from Gonzales to the March Convention, signer of Declaration of Independence, private at San Jacinto, where he was mortally wounded in the charge, died at DeZavalla's two days later; was attended by Dr. Labadie, who for want of proper facilities was unable to save him.

[79]

CAPTAIN ANDREW BRISCOE

Commanded Company A at San Jacinto, which had been recruited by Capt. Hy. Teal at San Angustine. Teal was sick, and Briscoe led in his place. After the war he lived at Harrisburg, where, in the forties, he projected the first railroad in Texas and did some grading with a purpose to build all the way from Harrisburg to California. Along his right-of-way the Southern Pacific runs today.

a nation. The wooden horse which Austin and other empresarios brought within the walls, which Spain had guarded for three centuries, had disgorged, and the way to the Pacific was open.

Whittier, the Quaker poet, who voiced the sentiments of those against expansion of our national limits, and the acquisition of more slave territory, sounded warning to Mexico:

> "Let the Sacramento herdsman
> Heed what sound the wind brings down
> Of footsteps on the crisping snow
> Of chill Nevada's crown,
> Full fast and hard the Saxon rides
> With rein of travel slack
> And bending o'er the saddle leaves
> The sunshine at his back."

JAMES W. FANNIN, JR.

Houston and San Jacinto; Travis and the Alamo; Fannin and Goliad; will ever be inalienably associated in our history.

Fannin was only thirty-one when he died, and though he may have erred in his military judgment, he left a name and fame which gathers luster with the passing years.

There were Fannings in the American Colonies for a century before the Revolution. At the beginning of that war Edmund Fanning was a lawyer in North Carolina, son-in-law of the Tory Governor Tryon, and generally obnoxious to the colonists. His brother James W. was an ardent patriot, and they went to war on opposite sides. When the war was over, Edmund Fanning followed the British flag into Canada, and for nineteen years was Governor of Prince Edward's Island and became a Lieutenant General in the British Army. His brother, James W., drifted down into Georgia and became an opulent planter. He was so intense in his partisanship for the Patriot cause, and so anxious not to be confused with his Tory brother that he dropped the "g" from his name, so that the world might know that though the Fannings may have been Tories, yet the Fannins were pure Patriots. James W. Fannin, Jr., as he signed himself even to the fatal day of his surrender to Urrea, was a grandson of old James W., who had died the year before James, Jr., was born.

When old James W. was gathered to his fathers in 1803, he left many sons and daughters, among them Isham S., who was a Major of Militia in the War of 1812. Major Fannin died in 1817, leaving his natural son James W. and his half-sister, an infant daughter, Eliza.

Eliza's mother was Margaret Porter, daughter of Oliver Porter, whom Isham Fannin had married in 1809.

James W.'s mother was named Walker, for in one of his letters to Major Belton in 1835 he says that he had entered West Point under the name of James W. Walker, this being the name of his maternal grandfather, who had adopted and reared him.

While young James was in West Point, 1819-21, his Cousin Martha Fannin was in a girls school in Philadelphia. She afterwards became the wife of Dr. Fort of Georgia, and left her "memories" for her children and grandchildren.

She says that her Cousin James, son of Uncle Isham, often visited her in Philadelphia, that he was a splendid, handsome young man, about her age. But she adds in retrospection, "He got into a fight in

MARTHA LOW FANNIN

Cousin of James W. Fannin, who fell at Goliad. No picture of Fannin has been found. Much of his early life is learned from recollections of this cousin, who became the wife of Dr. Fort, a distinguished Georgian.

West Point and left school, returning to Georgia, where he married. Then he went to Texas, where he lost his life."

Among her souvenirs was an aged clipping from a Georgia paper of 1836 telling of the massacre at Goliad.

James and his half-sister, Eliza, who was nearly fifteen years younger, grew up apart. Her mother married J. H. King of Morgan

ERASTUS (DEAF) SMITH

Leader of spy service for Houston's army was deaf and had poor eyesight. It was he who took five companions and destroyed Vince Bridge the day of the battle. Two days before he captured a courier carrying dispatches to Santa Anna. They were in a deer skin bag which had belonged to Travis, who was slain at the Alamo six weeks before. Smith married a Mexican woman and lived at Bexar when the Revolution began. He joined his countrymen, and his family fled in the Run Away Scrape. After the war the Congress of the Republic gave him the choice of a house in Bexar. He died in Richmond, Texas, in December, 1837.

City, Georgia, and while James was looked after, so he says, by his maternal grandfather Walker, Eliza had a stepfather and an Uncle William Porter who were kind to her. She was two years in a boarding school in Salem, North Carolina, 1828-1830, and Uncle William sent her to a girls school in New Haven, Connecticut, where she remained, 1830-1832.

James had entered West Point in 1819 when fourteen years, six months of age, so the record there shows. Two years later he had run away to Georgia and married.

PRIVATE BENJ. C. FRANKLIN

A private at San Jacinto and a District Judge under the Republic. Held the first District Court at Houston, Galveston and Brazoria. This picture was taken in his old age, for he was but a youth at San Jacinto. He joined Houston's army at Gonzales and during the retreat rode with Deaf Smith in the spy service.

In 1829, when Eliza was in Salem, her mother, then Margaret King, wrote her that Uncle William Porter had proposed to send her to the North to school, and the mother was very much in a quandary as to what Eliza should do. She put the question squarely to Eliza for decision (she was now nearly thirteen), and agreed to be reconciled to whatever Miss Eliza should decide. This was in September, but in December she wrote again, and with ample deference stated

WALTER P. LANE
(Fifty years later)

Walter P. Lane was an Irish lad of 19 when he fought as a private at San Jacinto, where he was wounded. He was an officer in the Mexican war twelve years later, and a Brigadier General in the Civil war. It was he who brought back for burial the bones of the Mier men which he gathered where they fell in Mexico. They were given sepulcher at LaGrange.

her opinion that it would not be wise for Eliza to go. She gave her reasons for this long-delayed decision.

"In the first place, it has always been my moste ernest indeavor to impress on your youthfull mind the importance of early piety, and the one thing needful genuine and true religion, and the fear of God which the scriptures of truth declare to be the beginning of wis-

HOUSTON AND HOCKLEY

Houston at the camp on the Lavaca dictating to Hockley the order to Captain Wm. T. Austin to go to Velasco and bring up the artillery.

dom. I have taken up an idea from general observation that young ladies educated at the North learn more of the shew and vainty of life while the more useful knowledge is almost, if not quite neglected."

In a postscript to this letter Eliza's mother adds: "I rec'd a letter from your brother James a few weeks since that they have a fine daughter and wish to be remembered to you."

Regardless of her mother's misgivings, Eliza went to New Haven for two years and braved the "shew and vainty of the North."

CAPTAIN ROBERT J. CALDER

Capt. Robert J. Calder commanded a company at San Jacinto which was recruited at Brazoria. The day after the battle he and Benjamin C. Franklin were sent with a message to President Burnet, who was on Galveston Island. They made the voyage from San Jacinto to Galveston in four days in a leaky rowboat.

Just before she left for this long stay she was in Georgia with her kinspeople, and on October 27, 1830, her half-brother James wrote her a long peculiar letter, which gives quite a vision of the temperament and character of young Fannin. He tells her reproachfully that he has heard from others that she is now with her mother and among her former friends, that he would like to consider himself "her dearest relative." "We have always been separated from each other, but you will not suspect me of selfishness or the want of that fraternal feeling incident to our relationship." After this passage he begins the discussion of some personal family matter, and tells her, "You are now of an age to know," but some careful hand has with knife or scissors neatly cut from the letter what she is now old enough to know. After the blank left by the censor's scissors, the letter continues for four pages, and refers to his "long silence, and peculiar situation." "If you cannot see this in all its true bearings, ask Mother or Mr. King." He urges her to visit him and joins in the extension of the invitation, "Your sister Minerva and your niece Missouri Pinckney." He grows eloquent in the description of his baby daughter whom Eliza has never seen. "To praise our little daughter would be useless. If you wish to see her or know anything of her, come and see her. I cannot visit my friends until after next year, when I hope to save enough money to buy a carriage, as we will then have too many to go any other way, and tho we do live down near the Indian border, we still have some pride."

In another letter about this time he speaks frankly and without reserve of his infant daughter. "I want you to see your only niece, Miss Missouri Pinckney. She is a real Fannin, and I do not say too much when I assert that she is one of the finest children in Georgia. She is all life, never cries, is always laughing."

In April, 1832, James is in Charleston, South Carolina, waiting for a packet to sail for Havana, and he spends an hour of his leisure in writing his sister, now at New Haven, a very long, very silly letter, full of boyish expressions. But for the firm, clear hand in which it is written, one would suspect that he was drinking when he wrote. He chides her for two pages for not having written often, and then such brief letters. "Writing, my own dear but truant sister is not only a relaxation from severe studies, but an amusement to the tired, worn-out mind—like a mile walk after a day's ride. It supplies the joints and sinews, makes many things vigorous and elastic. But my dear Eliza will not think that her only paternal brother is one of those crusty crabbed old crones who wishes to monopolize the whole of her time," etc.

After relaxing his mind in this lighter vein, he tells her that he left her sister Minerva and her nieces Missouri Pinckney and Eliza

CAPTAIN JUAN N. SEGUIN

Was a native Texan, and commanded a company of twenty Mexicans, most all native Texans who fought under Houston at San Jacinto. In after years he became embroiled with the American Texans at Bexar and was driven out and fought under Santa Anna in the war with the United States.

[90]

quite well, but does not pause to comment on the personality of the little daughters, though we hope he still regarded them the finest in Georgia.

A month later he wrote her again from Cuba. He is lonely among strangers, and his mind turns to his loved ones. "Feelings which seemed quite dormant yesterday are today in their zenith—nay, as warm as the tropic of Cancer will admit. I love my old friends with a holy love. No wonder then that I love my only sister a little."

GEORGE B. ERATH

Was a German emigrant, only 23 when he enlisted in Billingsly's company at Bastrop. When the Texans charged at San Jacinto he was alongside Lemuel Blakey; the Bastrop boy was killed; when Blakey fell Erath's gun had jammed, and he siezed Blakey's and kept on with the slaughter until sundown.

SANTA ANNA'S CAMP

A grove of ancient oaks which were old when Santa Anna camped under them 100 years ago. Here the dictator lay down for his afternoon siesta, and he relates, "When I was awakened they were rudely threatening my person with guns." Fifty feet from these oaks Castrillion was killed.

Again he turns to family scenes and refers to "my peculiar situation" and to the death of their father in touching, pathetic language.

"Can I (remember my peculiar situation) ever recur to the never to be forgotten April 26, 1817, and see our common parent in the last death struggle, and hear him calling for both of us, and you a helpless infant, unconscious of your loss, held in his dying arms; can I, who know a father's anxieties, witness this scene, remember this, and what he had done for me (which but few fathers would have done), not feel some solicitude for the object nearest his heart. The full overflowing heart of a true Fannin responds in feelings of deepest gratitude—in love the most lasting and indelible."

He tells her in this letter that he is going for a cargo of sugar, that he will keep a vessel in the trade, that he will be in New York in the summer and visit her in New Haven, and tell her a thousand things.

With the enthusiasm of a boy he relates that he has the finest collection of shells "you have ever seen—nay, ever read about." That he has bought two parrots, two guinea pigs, and various other odd creatures, including two blue-headed ring-striped pigeons, all for her.

Though he has much to say of his feelings and his souvenirs, he makes scant mention of his business. He was now embarking in the contraband slave trade. Though slavery then and for forty years after prevailed in the South, and slaves were freely bought and sold, yet the United States and other nations had forbidden their further importation from Africa. The result was that there was a great industry in bringing cargoes of negroes from Africa and smuggling them into the Southern States, where the planters gladly bought them. Many of these slave traders had stations in the West Indies where they would sell to venturesome dealers who would peddle them out along the coast.

While slavery and the slave trade is looked on now as an outlawed enterprise, yet in those days the people of the South were slave owners, and most of them believed in what they called our peculiar institution, and were glad to keep in touch with a reliable trader from whom they could get slaves at a reasonable price. James

CAPTAIN MOSLEY BAKER

Capt. Mosley Baker joined Houston's army while it was on the Colorado, and retreated with him to San Felipe. When Houston retreated to Groce's, Baker would not follow, but remained there. On Houston's order, he burned San Felipe and then crossed the river and camped on the east bank, where he remained and disputed the crossing with Santa Anna.

BATTLE OF SAN JACINTO

The sixteenth decisive battle in the world's history, and was the direct means of spreading Saxon sovereignty from the Sabine to the Pacific. It accomplished the freedom of Texas, and led to the Mexican war, where we acquired Arizona, New Mexico, Nevada, California, Utah and portions of Colorado, Wyoming, Kansas and Oklahoma.

Bowie was a slave trader, and many other names prominent in our early annals were directly or indirectly interested in this enterprise.

Texas was then beginning to attract wide attention as a plantation and possible stock country, and two years after James' first expedition to Cuba, when he bought the parrots and blue-headed, ring-striped pigeons, we find him extending his operations to the Texas coast.

Details are meager as to just when Fannin first came to Texas,

R. M. WILLIAMSON

Three-Legged Willie, the Patrick Henry of the Revolution. Lawyer, judge, and private soldier at San Jacinto. He rode into battle wearing a coonskin cap, ornamented with coon tails. He was crippled in the knee, and used a wooden stump on which he rested his wounded knee.

but we know that he made a voyage to the mouth of the Brazos with a small cargo of negroes in June, 1834.

On the 26th day of May in that year he was in Havana, where he made a contract with Harvey Kendrick for the purchase from one Thompson of the schooner Crawford for $5000.00, for which he drew a draft on E. W. Gregory of New Orleans. The original of this

GENERAL SANTA ANNA

Seeing all was lost, he and his fifty horsemen rode hard toward Harrisburg, followed by Capt. Karnes and a small squad of mounted riflemen, who slew many of the fugitives. When he reached Vince Bayou and found the bridge destroyed, he left his horse and took to the woods, and was captured the next day.

[97]

contract with its interesting recitals is on file among the papers in probate in Brazoria County. It recites that Thompson and Henshaw of New Orleans are the owners of the boat, and "that it is to sail from Havana on June 12th, coming with a cargo of *sixteen free negroes* which is shown and made manifest by the oath of James W. Fannin, Jr., before the United States Consul at Havana, together with some two or three gentlemen passengers for the port or roadstead of the Brassos in the province of Texas on the coast of Mexico

EL PRESIDENTE SANTA ANNA

When he was brought in a prisoner the day after the battle, he was recognized by his men, who excitedly called out, "El Presidente." Taken before General Houston, who was wounded, the Mexican Dictator admitted his identity, and began to bargain for his freedom.

where the blacks are to be landed and the schooner is to proceed at once for New Orelans." Payment for the boat was to be made in New Orleans.

The "*free negroes* and two or three gentlemen passengers" were no doubt duly unloaded at the Brassos roadstead, but Fannin must have failed to realize enough cash out of the transaction to settle his debt for the boat. On August 22nd he was in Mobile and wrote Thompson asking for further indulgence and offering to get an endorsement from Edward Hanrick of Mobile, "who is to be interested with me in the next trip."

He made fair promises to Thompson, as debtors usually do, and said he would pay the debt if he had to sell a drove of valuable mules he had in Louisiana.

Of course, these *free negroes* were a myth. Mexico did not recognize slavery and under the letter of Mexican law, slaves could not be introduced into the Republic. So it was necessary to make an oath before the Consul at Havana that these African blacks just bought no doubt in the Cuban slave mart were free persons being transported to the Mexican coast.

Thompson evidently granted an extension of Fannin's debt, for more than a year later we find Fannin writing him again, making further excuses and asking additional indulgence. This letter is dated San Barnardo, Province of Texas, September 15, 1835. He tells Mr. Thompson, "I have been lying ill—nay, nearly dead." After various excuses and promises he says: "I have since made a good trip, having bought for myself and others 152 negroes in May last (1835), but cannot realise any cash for them until March or April when you shall be fully paid every cent I owe you. You need not be concerned about the present state of affairs in Texas. There is no serious danger for us. Tho we may have to fight some little—but success will certainly follow our efforts. * * * I am settled on Caney Creek, midway between Brasoria and Matagorda."

This letter was written in September and in October Captain Fannin had mustered the Brazoria guards and marched to Gonzales to take part in the first campaign of the Revolution, where he did "some little fighting."

[99]

The debt Fannin owed Thompson for the schooner Crawford was only one of many that pressed him in those days. He had a leaky pen when he came to signing notes and drafts, and when he located in Texas in 1834-5 he left a trail of such obligations all the way from Georgia. Among the claims filed with his administrator were notes made as far back at 1828, contracts unfulfilled, including the balance due for the boat Crawford, drafts which had been protested in Mobile and New Orleans.

SANTA ANNA AT 55

He returned home after the war in Texas, and was for a time in retirement, but was again and again President of Mexico. He lost his leg in a skirmish with French soldiers at Vera Cruz in 1838, and had his amputated limb buried with much ceremony. In an uprising against him in 1844 a mob dug up the leg and dragged it through the streets.

He was in Havana in January, 1835, where he drew a draft for $5000.00 on St. John & Leovans of Mobile. This found its way to John A. Merle & Company of New Orleans.

In April, 1835, Fannin was in New Orleans, when he was arrested for debt at the instance of Theopholus Hyde, to whom he owed $3000.00, and one Kenan procured his release by paying $1500.00. Three years later Kenan's executor filed a claim against Fannin's administrator for the amount of this and other debts.

GENERAL FILISOLA WAS AN ITALIAN

General Filisola was on the Brazos at Fort Bend with more than 2000 men when the Battle of San Jacinto was fought. Santa Anna, at the dictation of General Houston, sent Filisola orders to retreat to Bexar, and he took the short route via Goliad for the Rio Grande.

John A. Merle filed an affidavit with Fannin's administrator that he had lost the draft which Fannin drew in Havana; that he had received it on October 16, 1835, and placed it in a strong iron box at his mercantile house in New Orleans when on that same night robbers broke into the house and broke open the strong iron box and took out the contents—that afterwards some of the papers were found in a wallet on a boat in the Mississippi River. But the draft afterwards turned up, and with a flock of others found its way to the files on poor Fannin's estate.

Among others of this prolific flock was a note for $445.00 which Fannin gave one S. Whitting at some place not named on July 10, 1835. When Whitting filed this note with Fannin's administrator in 1836 he refused payment under an oath that it was without consideration, and was given in payment of a gambling debt which Fannin owed Whitting, all of which Whitting stoutly denied.

On January 12, 1836, just before Fannin went down the coast to Copano and Goliad he made an ambitious contract with Joseph Mims of Brazoria, which is interesting as it marks the close of his dubious business career. It recites that Mims owned 3000 acres of land on the San Bernard; that he had eight negroes, men and boys, sixty head of cattle, two yoke of oxen and carts and yokes, four work mules and two horses, five ploughs and gear, three hundred bushels of corn, eighty head of hogs. All these lands and chattels he put into a farming partnership with Fannin at a valuation of $25,000.00. Fannin put in twenty-three African negroes, to wit, twelve men, seven women and four boys, valued at $17,250.00. He bound himself to pay Mims the difference of $7750.00 in five equal installments, "But should the tranquility of the country authorize it, said Fannin is at liberty to pay the whole debt in negroes at a fair valuation."

These business details arranged, Col. Fannin hurried down the coast and took command of the Georgia and Alabama and other volunteers who were coming into Texas to aid in the Revolution. Sixty days later his command was captured by Urrea and he and his men fell before a firing squad.

"The some little fighting" which he had predicted in his letter to Thompson the previous September had come to pass.

THE PHANTOM DR. HARRISON

A Story of the Goliad Campaign

Our first glimpse of Doctor Harrison is from the diary of Fairfax Gray, who came into Texas early in the year of 1836 to negotiate a loan to the Revolutionary Government, which was organized at Washington on the Brazos in March of that year.

In those troubled days there was no newspaper published in Texas. When Santa Anna's Army approached San Felipe, the Bordens suspended their weekly paper, and it was not published again until in the following autumn, when the capital was established at Columbia.

Fairfax Gray was not in the army. He was at Washington on the Brazos when the provisional government was set up, and when President Burnet and the members of his interim cabinet left for Harrisburg as Santa Anna came galloping into the heart of the colonies. Gray went along with them and each day he made a faithful note of what he saw and heard, and his diary is one of the most interesting and dependable sources of information about those stormy days.

Houston camped on the Brazos for three weeks after the interim government and Fairfax Gray fled to Harrisburg. Gray reached that place about April 1, and mingled with the refugees along the bayou. Hundreds of people from the plantations on the Brazos and Colorado were hurrying this way headed for the Louisiana border. At one time there were 5000 people waiting to cross the Lynchburg Ferry. Steamboats were plying up and down the bayou going out to Galveston and along the coast.

On April 15, Fairfax Gray was at Lynchburg, and after an exciting day wrote two pages in his loquacious diary:

"This morning rode out to meet the President. * * * A great number of fugitives are still passing. One lady from the West was delivered in a canebrake on her flight. * * * At night the steamboat came down, and on it all the inhabitants of Harrisburg.

Doctor Harrison also came on the steamboat, the son of Gen. William H. Harrison, who was reported to have been massacred at Victoria. He was taken prisoner, but General Urrea, having been minister from Mexico to Columbia at the time that General Harrison was also a minister there from the United States, out of respect and regard for the father, he protected the son. He was entertained in General's tent and was permitted to return to the United States, on parole. The

WILLIAM FAIRFAX GRAY

Of Virginia was in Texas during the San Jacinto campaign, and wrote daily in a diary which covered the first 90 days of 1836, and is one of the most valuable sources of the history of that period. He afterwards practiced law in Houston, and his son, Peter W. Gray, who began practice here in 1842, was a distinguished lawyer for 30 years, and was a Justice of the Supreme Court of Texas.

General, on his departure, gave him a fine riding horse, $100, a cloak, and permission to bring off an American prisoner as a servant. He brought off Ben Mordaci of Richmond, Va., who was thereby saved from the general massacre that took place of Fannin's men. Colonel Garay conducted him away from the Mexican camp, and at parting gave him a sword. He speaks highly of Urrea and of Garay—latter is Governor of Durango and commands the Southern Division of the invading army. Siezma (Sesma) commands the center, which is now at San Felipe. The Northern Division is destined for Nacogdoches, and Harrison says the report in camp was that this division had proceeded up the Colorado 300 miles without meeting a white man. It will strike across the upper country to Nacogdoches. He says Urrea was very indignant at the massacre of Fannin's troops, said it was done without his orders or knowledge, and that he intended to resign his command and return to his government as soon as the army reached Brazoria. Speaks highly of Garay. He confirms the report of a revolution in Mexico which had caused the return of Santa Anna."

This is all that the diarist says in this entry about Dr. Harrison. But he continues:

"I also saw Captain Holland, who was an officer in Fannin's artillery. He escaped the massacre by his prowess and courage. Captain Wallis was his file leader. Suspecting what was about to happen from his knowledge of the language, he proposed to Wallis that they should make an effort to escape. Wallis declined and said, 'Let us meet our fate like men.' But Holland watched his opportunity, knocked down one Mexican, jostled and overturned and ran over a second and seized the scopet of a third, wrested it from him, knocked him down, and in the confusion that ensued ran off. To his surprise and dismay he found there was an outer line of guards, one of whom raised his scopet to shoot him. Holland at once lowered his gun and shot off the fellow's skull, dashed the scopet on him, and continued his flight without any further interruption. He suffered much in an attempt to reach the settlements. Nine of Fannin's men are known to have escaped. I this day bought a horse of George B. Wilson for $50, and am ready to start."

Thus ends the faithful Fairfax's narrative of the 15th.

DR. JOSEPH H. BARNARD

Was in Dr. Shackelford's company at Goliad and was spared the massacre. He afterwards made the first list of the men who fought and fell with Fannin. The exact number of men with Fannin will never be known, but from Dr. Barnard's list, and later checks, it is certain that at least 390 men were in the massacre; about 60 were spared or escaped.

DR. JACK SHACKELFORD

Early in 1836 several companies of volunteer soldiers recruited in the Southern States landed on the gulf coast and joined Fannin at Goliad. Dr. Shackelford, of Courdtland, Alabama, commanded one called the Red Rovers. He was saved from the massacre with the other physicians, but his son and his nephew were slain. He returned to Alabama, where he died.

The opening entry of Saturday, April 16, reads:

"The steamboat went down (the bayou) this morning with the members of the cabinet in it, and Dr. Harrison on his way to the United States."

The passengers on this boat which reached Lynchburg on the night of the 15th and "went down" on the early morning of the 16th, brought news that Mexican troops had reached Harrisburg. It was this information which prompted the purchase of the horse from George Wilson, and, true to his recitation of readiness to start in the closing entry of the 15th, Fairfax Gray was on his way to the Louisiana border "after breakfast" on Saturday, the 16th.

A search of the records of Fannin's men shows that there was no Dr. Harrison enlisted in any of the several companies which composed the ill-fated army. The names of the doctors who were saved are well known. They were Dr. Shackleford of the Red Rovers; Dr. Bernard, Dr. Fields, but no Dr. Harrison.

Ben H. Modaci was a private in Captain Bullock's company of Georgia troops, and is marked "escaped."

At that time General Harrison was one of the most prominent figures in the United States, and in that year he was the Whig candidate for President of the United States, but was defeated by Martin Van Buren. Four years later (1840) he defeated Van Buren, and became the ninth President.

Among the papers of President Lamar (recently published) is the original of a letter from James W. Robinson to President Burnet, dated April 6, 1836. At that time Burnet was at Harrisburg. On that day Mosley Baker, with 40 men, after burning San Felipe, had crossed the Brazos and camped on the opposite bank, where they watched Santa Anna march into San Felipe on the 8th and out again on the 9th. Houston's army was then up the river at Groce's.

Robinson, who had lately been Lieutenant Governor of the First Provisional Government, and Acting Governor after the impeachment of Henry Smith, was then a private in Mosley Baker's company. He had come to Texas from Ohio a few years before, and had known General Harrison, who was for a long time Governor of the Territory of Indiana.

Governor Robinson's letter follows:

To His Excellency, D. G. Burnet
President of the Republic of Texas
Camp Opposite the Ruins of San Felipe, April 6, 1836.

This moment information has been received here that Colonel Fannin surrendered on the express condition that they should march back to Goliad and lay down their arms and pass their parol of honor not to fight against Mexico during the present war, that they should then forthwith be sent to New Orleans by way of Copano at the expense of Mexico, which conditions were not complied with. On the contrary, company after company were ordered out and shot. So say four out of the first company who fell down among the dead and afterwards ran away, there being no cavalry present, made their escape. * * * Thus the whole of the men and officers that were surrendered by Colonel Fannin are now among the dead, shamefully murdered in utter contempt and violation of an article of capitulation and the usages of civilized and Christian nations. It is my solemn opinion that you ought to make this atrocious act of punic faith known at the City of Washington to our agents there, and ask the recognition of our independence and the protection of the United States. If done at all, it is important that it be done soon, as the Congress will probably adjourn next month. * * *

General William Henry Harrison had a son, Doctor Harrison, recently inhumanly butchered at Victoria, who was not in arms or in any hostile attitude whatsoever. * * * It would be well to inform his father of his melancholy fate, and ask his interference in our behalf. "He was literally cut to pieces on a log like a mess of pork," so says my informant, just arrived from the scene of slaughter, where two or three other North Americans shared his fate. * * * James W. Robinson.

This letter of April 6, if delivered to Burnet, must have reached him at Harrisburg about the same time that "Doctor Harrison" came, for they were both in Lynchburg on April 15.

Herman Ehrenberg, one of the survivors of the massacre, gives quite a lively narrative of Doctor Harrison, who was with Urrea when Ehrenberg was recaptured on the Navidad. He says Harrison was found by Mexican cavalry somewhere in the Guadalupe Valley, and soon won the favor of Urrea; that "he was a very peculiar person, and up to this time (1842) his appearance in the prairie has been a riddle. That he was not the son of old General Harrison has long

JAMES W. ROBINSON

Had left Ohio with "another woman," in 1828, abandoning his family there. He came to the consultation as a delegate from Nacogdoches. Smith, who was a good but dull man, full of egotism, and given to bombast, started a fuss with the council which led to an ugly scandalous wrangle, which went on all fall. The council impeached Governor Smith and Robinson assumed to act until the convention met in March. After the convention he joined Houston's army and fought as a private at San Jacinto. He wrote President Burnet that Dr. Harrison had been cut to pieces on a log like a mess of pork.

been proven, but who he was and why he was wandering around alone in the Wild West is yet to be solved."

He says that Doctor Harrison persuaded Urrea to issue an amnesty proclamation to the colonists, and to send him ahead to present it to them.

He writes at length an account of how he addressed a gathering of colonists, telling them of the greatness and goodness of Urrea, and how the colonists heckled him and ridiculed him and made ready to ride him on an 18-foot rail, and how the doctor talked them out of it and scampered on east.

Ehrenberg was much impressed with the shrewd Yankee, as he calls him, and concluded his narrative:

"In his narrow-shouldered figure and Lord's prayer face the gigantic and ever-active force of the Yankee nation lived.

"This Doctor X, as we may call him, disappeared, and no one ever heard who he was, what he was, where he went or from whence he came."

The stirring events of the San Jacinto campaign which ended in the battle of April 21 at Lynchburg, wiped out for a time many of the details that had gone before, and Doctor Harrison was forgotten.

The only trace of him after he went down on the steamboat on the morning of April 16, about the time Fairfax Gray left for Louisiana on the horse he bought from Wilson, is a short notice under the heading "Texas Items," published in the Louisiana Courier June 21, 1836:

"Young Zavala and Doctor Harrison (son of General Harrison) came as passengers on the Good Hope."

At that time General Harrison was a candidate for President of the United States, and was one of the best known men in all North America. Next to General Jackson he was the outstanding living character in the States. That the presence of his son in Texas, and his awful fate, or his miraculous escape, would attract so little attention, seemed marvelous. Other men from the States who returned from Texas during these stormy days told and retold their experiences and their names and exploits found their way into print. But not so with Doctor Harrison or Ben Mordaci.

What became of his servant Mordaci?

[111]

He was living in Victoria in 1840 when the Comanches made their awful raid to the coast, and was a victim of their wrath. The *Colorado Citizen,* published at Matagorda, carried a news item in August, 1840, that B. H. Mordaci, late of this place, was killed on the Garcitas River by the Comanches.

But what about Doctor Harrison? No one ever claimed any land for his services, and in all the subsequent annals of early Texas there is no mention of his name.

General Urrea published a diary of his Texas campaign after he returned to Mexico (1837), and a search of it reveals the following:

After his great victory at Goliad in March, and the massacre of Fannin's men on Palm Sunday, he pushed on east to Victoria and Matagorda, and was camped on the Colorado at Cayce's Crossing on April 9.

"On that day," he notes, "I sent young Doctor Harrison, my prisoner, the son of a general of the United States, to the colonies with the special mission of speaking to the colonists who had not taken up arms, offering them guarantees and the protection of the army. It will be seen that this measure was not fruitless."

The entry on April 22 recites:

"I marched into Brazoria at 10 a. m. Many English, American and German colonists awaited me there with their families as a result of the commission I had given Doctor Harrison on the Colorado to allay their fears. They expressed satisfaction with the treatment accorded them.   *   *   *   They offered to turn Galveston Island over to me.   *   *   *   It is a homage due to justice to confess that Doctor Harrison had contributed very decisively to the good disposition that was noticeable among the colonists. He thought on his part that he owed me his life, and omitted no means to express his gratitude, even to the extent of risking it a second time because he thought he owed it to me."

On April 23 Urrea was about to descend on Galveston Island, where there were a thousand refugees (among them Doctor Harrison), when he received "a mysterious message from General Filisola" telling of a disaster to Santa Anna on the 21st.

Fairfax Gray's diary lay unpublished for 70 years. Herman Ehrenberg's memoirs were published in a foreign language, and he was later killed by Indians in Arizona. Urrea's diary was not published in English until 1929, and Doctor Harrison was a forgotten tale.

Excited by these conflicting reports as to his identity and his fate, I decided to find out more about him. So, in 1929 I wrote Russell B. Harrison of Indianapolis, son of Benjamin Harrison, the twenty-third President, who was a grandson of Gen. William Henry Harrison, the ninth President, to know if his great-grandfather had a son who was a doctor, and if so, was this doctor in Texas in the days of the Revolution.

I had a prompt reply from him that he was well informed about the Harrison family, and knew its history since the days of Oliver Cromwell and the Restoration, nearly 300 years before; that his great-grandfather had no doctor son, and none of his sons was in Texas at any time. To prove his positive assertion, if proof were necessary, he gave the names of the five children of the ninth President, and the date of birth of each, and when and where each died. There were three sons, John Cleve, who died in 1830; William Henry, a lawyer, who died in 1838, and John Scott, who was his father's father.

This accurate information from the son of the illustrious family confirmed Herman Ehrenberg's suspicions and mine, and upon proof which would have proved the issue in any court, I wrote in my "History of the San Jacinto Campaign" (published in 1930) that Doctor Harrison was a myth.

Later I had occasion to make a careful study of the Harrison family for a sketch of the lives of our thirty Presidents which I prepared for broadcasting. It is one of the most illustrious in American history. Benjamin Harrison, father of the ninth President, was Governor of Virginia and a signer of the Declaration of Independence. He was descended from Thomas Harrison, one of the Generals in Cromwell's army, and one of the judges who condemned Charles I to die. His father was a butcher at New Castle. When Charles II became King of England he seized upon the regicides, and Thomas Harrison was one of the first to fall into his royal clutches, and the first victim of his right royal wrath.

[113]

Samuel Pepys, like Fairfax Gray, wrote a diary (but it is neither so well written nor so interesting), and, like Fairfax, he made a note about the Harrison family. The entry of October 13, 1660, reads:

"I went to Charing Cross today to see Major General Thomas Harrison hanged, drawn and quartered, which was done there, he looking as cheerful as a man could do in that condition. He was presently cut down and his head and heart shown the people, at which there were great shouts of joy. It is said that he said he was sure to come shortly at the right hand of Christ to judge them that now judged him, and that his wife do now expect his coming again. Thus it was my chance to see the King beheaded at Whitehall and to see the first blood shed in revenge at Charing Cross."

What Samuel Pepys saw done to Thomas Harrison on October 13, 1660, was just what Governor Robinson's informant assured him had been done to Doctor Harrison at Victoria in March, 1836. It hardly seems probable that he got the events confused.

In my Harrison research I found that President John Quincy Adams had sent General Harrison as our minister to the new revolutionary Republic of Columbia in 1826, where he served for a time, and that General Urrea was at that same time Mexican minister there.

I found that H. Montgomery had written and published a biography of General Harrison in 1852. In a carefully prepared appendix he gave an account of the death and funeral of the ninth President, giving the names of the members of the family present and those absent, and the children who died before. He lists the three sons named by Russell B. Harrison and two others:

"J. C. S. Harrison, who married Miss Pike (both dead)," and Dr. Benjamin Harrison, a son who died in 1840.

Following this information in Montgomery's biography, I developed the following facts:

The *La Advertiser* of April 13, 1836, published in New Orleans, published an account of the butchery of Dr. Harrison very much as Governor Robinson gave it in his letter to Burnet, and says that it came from Colonel Horton, whose cavalry were at Goliad the day of Fannin's last fight, and who escaped.

The *Cincinnati Commercial* of April 30, 1836, republished this item. On May 20, 1836, the Cincinnati paper carried an item that at the local theatre the Texas Battle Cry was being sung, and that an altar was to be erected on the stage which would bear the names of the martyrs Travis, Crockett, Bowie, *and Harrison.*

An old volume of letters from General Harrison written in 1833 and 1834, which recently came into my hands, contains one to Tipton in which he refers to "my son Benjamin who is on a trapping expedition on the Big Horn River," and another to Tipton, May, 1834, "To my astonishment and great regret my son Benjamin returned from the Rocky Mountains. * * * In his trip he squandered a thousand dollars in a way wholly unaccountable." This was two years before the Goliad campaign.

The *Cincinnati Gazette* of June 19, 1840, carries this notice:

"Died on Tuesday evening last June 16 at North Bend, Dr. Benjamin Harrison, son of General Harrison, in the 34th year of his age."

A recent visit to the family burial ground of the Harrisons at North Bend disclosed a marble slab bearing this inscription:

Erected in Memory of
Dr. Benjamin Harrison, Son of
William Henry and Ann Harrison
Born September 8, 1806
Died June 17, 1840
at North Bend

From this information we may conclude, Russell Harrison to the contrary notwithstanding, that General Harrison had a doctor son; that he was a wanderer and somewhat prodigal; that he was in all probability in Texas in 1836; and that he sleeps in the family burial ground at North Bend.

ASA WALKER, WHO FELL AT THE ALAMO

All the world has heard the story of the Alamo and about Colonel Travis, Davy Crockett, Bonham and Bowie, who fell there in the early morning of March 6, 1836, when Castrillion led the assault, while Santa Anna looked on and the Mexican band played the assassin's song.

There were 180 others who died that day along with Travis and Crockett and Bonham and Bowie, whose names are known only to the student who digs deep into the records of a long past. Like the soldiers at San Jacinto and those who fell with Fannin, most of them were very young, many of them mere boys who had come into Texas to gratify youth's fancy for a fling at the game of war. The average age was thirty, and the oldest was fifty. There were twelve boys under twenty-one.

When Bexar was captured in December and the Mexicans expelled, it looked as if the war were over, and these young warriors left with no more worlds to conquer. Most of them tramped down the Goliad Road to join Fannin, or Dr. Grant, or Frank Johnson, all of whom were promising them a march into Mexico. A few stragglers, probably a hundred, loitered in San Antonio, where Captain Neill kept a kind of military organization under authority from the weak Colonial Council at San Felipe. Later he left, and the Colonial Government named Travis to succeed him, but James Bowie claimed the command.

It was well understood that a Mexican Army would be back on this battle front in the spring, and Travis planned that Bexar would be the rallying place of the Texans, who would mass here to hold this important place.

Among those present was young Asa Walker, a youth of twenty-three. He had left Columbia, Tennessee, in the summer of 1835, and come to Cole's Settlement at Washington on the Brazos, and was indebted to William W. Gant of that place for money advanced for the trip. Shortly after his arrival the battle cry was raised for volunteers to march to Bexar to expel the Mexican General Cos, who held that place, and Walker went to Gant's house to consult with him about the venture.

The New Orleans Greys, a small company of infantry recruited in that city, and commanded by Captain Thomas H. Breese, had just passed through on its way to Bexar, all in uniform, and bearing a flag, which became the flag of the Alamo, and this had helped arouse the ardor of the countryside.

Not finding Gant at home, and finding Gant's overcoat and gun, he took them and left two scraps of paper. One a note: "Due William W. Gant $35.87½, the amount of my expenses from Columbia, Tennessee, to this place. Given under my hand and seal this November 28, 1835, at Washington Department of Brazos. Asa Walker." One wonders how the one-half cent balance was arrived at; Gant evidently expected to be paid in full.

The following is a facsimile of the letter:

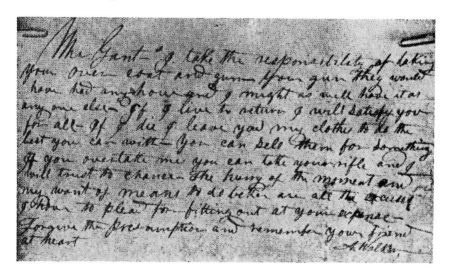

Mexican friends of Travis warned him almost daily during February of the approach of the enemy; that the army had passed the Rio Grande, but he professed to disbelieve their reports. When pressed by Rodrigues, who was in sympathy with the Texans, to retreat, he replied that he and his men had decided to stay and die in the Alamo.

They were scattered about the town when John W. Smith and Dr. John Sutherland were dispatched on fleet horses to reconnoitre down the Laredo Road, and when they came riding back under whip and spur, with word that the enemy's cavalry was just over the hill, the Texans rushed to the Alamo and began preparing for its defense.

It was the old mission fortress San Antonio Valerio, which had been established on the bank of the river by Governor Alercon, one hundred and eighteen years before. Nearby was the presidio of San Antonio, which had been maintained as a garrison since 1718. Just below was the Villa San Fernando de Bexar, which had been a civil settlement for one hundred years. Across the river and below was the chain of deserted missions, where many long-vanished tribes had faded away under the wasting influences of the white man's ways. It had come to be called Alamo from the cottonwood trees which had grown about it. Adjoining the chapel was a stone wall enclosing about two acres, such fortifications being a part of all the frontier missions. The walls were four feet thick. Here in the cloister many a weary Franciscan priest had knelt in prayer as he passed on pilgrimages from Mexico to the eastern missions. From its watchtowers generations of padres had scanned the horizon to detect the ever-threatened approach of the Apache and Comanche, and had seen in the distance the signal smokes of the red invaders.

The Mexicans occupying the town unfurled a black flag from the cathedral steeple on Main plaza, half a mile away. The Texans displayed the flag which the New Orleans Greys brought with them in November. Herman Ehrenberg, who was one of them, says it was presented as they crossed the Sabine: "That the tender hand of a fair Texan gave us in the name of the beauties of the land a blue silk flag bearing the inscription 'To the first company of Texas volunteers from New Orleans'." This flag is now in the National Museum in the City of Mexico.

But in the face of the common danger which unmistakably spelled doom to the defenders, there was dissention and a divided command. Though Travis came with authority from the Colonial Government, James Bowie, who returned from Goliad in January with thirty men, was looked upon as commander of the volunteers. About half the now 140 men were classed as regulars, and half as volunteers, and the two commanders clashed all day long.

Bowie, without consulting Travis, undertook to open a parley with the Mexicans and sent a note under a flag of truce, which was answered with insolence. Just at this time Colonel Bowie was suddenly seized with typhoid pneumonia, and took to his bed, where he died in the final assault on March 6th.

He was an interesting person, a small man, reticent and modest, slow in speech, but quick with knife and gun. He had come into Texas about sixteen years before, when LaFitte, the pirate, was operating his slave market on Galveston Island, and engaged in the contraband slave trade. He would buy negroes from the pirate ships at $1.00 per pound, and smuggle them into Louisiana, where he would sell them for high prices. In this way he made a considerable fortune, and took up his residence at San Antonio, where he married the daughter of Vermandi. During the thirteen days of the siege he lay desperately ill and was slain on his couch.

During these thirteen days the garrison of young almost boy soldiers lived on corn and beef, which was poorly prepared, for there was no commissary.

Asa Walker had many companions near his own age. His cousin, Jacob Walker, who was thirty-one, had come into Texas the year before and settled at Nacogdoches. He and Jacob renewed their comradeship here. Jacob was the last man killed. Of the 183 men, 32 were from Tennessee, Asa's native state. There were 33 from the British Isles, all quite young. Fourteen English lads, nine Irish, and four Scotch, and two Welch boys. Most all of these men were in their twenties. One of the Scotchmen, John McGregor, had his bagpipe, and when there was a lull in the fighting he would fetch his bagpipe and Davy Crockett his fiddle and they would vie with each other in the noise they could make.

There was one group of young men who had left Kentucky a few months before. Peter James Bailey, a lawyer, 24; Daniel William Cloud, 22; William Turtelroy, 22; Archer Thomas, 19; Joe Washington, 28. They had passed through Nacogdoches on January 14th, where they took the oath of allegiance to Texas, and walked all the way to Bexar, where they sealed that oath with their blood and their young lives.

There were the three Taylor brothers from Liberty, Texas: Edward, 18; James, 20; George, 22.

Charles W. Haskell, of Nashville, Tennessee, was Asa's own age. He and his cousin, C. R. Haskell, had left School in Tennessee to follow Captain Duval's Kentucky Company to Texas in the previous autumn. They were together at Goliad when General Houston made his famous visit to Refugio in February, and he sent Charles W. with a dispatch to Travis directing him to blow up the Alamo and fall back beyond the Guadalupe. After delivering the message Charles remained to die in the Alamo, and his cousin, C. R., was massacred at Goliad twenty days later. Haskell County is named for these lads.

Long before Santa Anna's troops arrived, Travis began sending couriers for help, and his sometimes frantic and always bold messages reached all parts of the colonies. Twenty or more messengers bearing these dispatches escaped. Bonham sent twice to Fannin at Goliad for help, rode back into the beleagued garrison in the last days of the siege to die with his comrades.

The only survivors were Mrs. Dickinson and her infant daughter, wife and daughter of one of the fallen soldiers, and Joe, a negro servant of Travis. They were sent on east with the terrible tidings. Joe became famous as the bearer of the first news to the Texans. After the war Edwin Waller became administrator of Travis' estate, and took over Joe. The following year Joe, hearing his people could be free in Mexico, ran away, and though Administrator Waller advertised for many months, he was never heard from.

The bodies of the slain were piled and burned, Asa Walker with all the rest, and the invading army went marching on to San Jacinto.

After the war, when the first election was called for members of Congress of the Republic, Mr. William W. Gant came out of his hiding and was elected to Congress, and bravely served his people on the floor of the house. He carefully preserved Asa's note for $35.87½ and the letter agreeing to pay for the overcoat and gun. He took out letters of administration on Asa's estate, and presented the note and a claim for twenty dollars for the coat and thirty-five

SAM HOUSTON

First President of the Republic of Texas. Elected in September, 1836, and inaugurated in October, when he took over the administration from Burnet, who had been head of the ad-interim government. Under the Constitution of the Republic a President could not serve two consecutive terms, and in 1838 he was succeeded by Lamar, but at the close of Lamar's term Houston was chosen again.

for the gun. He had certificates issued for Asa's military service, and land located, nearly 4000 acres, and then had this land sold to satisfy his debt of $90.87½. Asa Walker paid Gant for his passage, the overcoat and gun with his young life.

THE REPUBLIC OF TEXAS

It lasted two weeks less than ten years. Its days were filled with wars and rumors of war. There was intermittent war with Mexico, which never recognized Texas independence. There was intermittent war with the Indian tribes, who clung to their homes and hunting grounds. But a constant stream of new people flowed into its forests and onto its prairies. Old Baron Bastrop's vision of one hundred thousand Texans was now to be realized.

The country between the Nueces and the Rio Grande remained wild, alternately swept by Mexican bandits and marauding Indians, with a sprinkling of bad men from Texas and the States. The frontier line of the colonies, which had been the old Spanish Trail, was pushed north, but every mile was measured with an Indian massacre.

Twice Mexican armies came as far as Bexar, but each time hurried back to the border with the Texans on their heels. Twice the Texans tried an offensive with disastrous results.

MIRABEAU BONAPARTE LAMAR

Second President of the Republic, commanded the cavalry at San Jacinto, a poet and a dreamer, with visions of an empire. He came of a distinguished Georgia family, and was an uncle of L. Q. C. Lamar, afterwards known as the "Great Mississippian."

The Santa Fe Expedition of 1841 went out with the approval of President Lamar to set up a government and open trade with Santa Fe, which was claimed to be in Texas territory. It went with soldiers and traders, who, after weary months across a thousand miles of roadless mountains, desert and plain, fell into the hands of the Mexican Governor Arimijo, who confiscated their goods and sent the survivors on foot another thousand miles to Mexico City, where they were put in dungeons.

DR. ANSON JONES

The last President of the Republic, furled the flag of Texas at Austin in February, 1846, and unfurled the Stars and Stripes. He retired to private life and brooded over the ingratitude of his people. He took his life in the old Capitol Hotel at Houston in 1857.

[124]

An answer to this "friendly" expedition were two Mexican raids on Bexar the next year, which came and went in a gallop. An answer to these raids was a Texas raid on the border and across the river to Mier, where Colonel Fisher and his men were captured and started down to Mexico to join the Santa Fe prisoners. When they got below Saltillo they revolted, mobbed the guards, and got away. But it was a long, long way back to the border, and they wandered in the mountains and were retaken and returned to the place from which they revolted.

As a matter of discipline, and on orders from Santa Anna, who was again President of Mexico, the guards set up a death lottery and a jar was filled with beans one-tenth black, and those who drew black beans were shot at sundown the same day. Those who had the good fortune to draw white were marched on. Together with the Santa Fe prisoners and many taken in the raids on Bexar, there were several hundred Texans who were housed in the old Prison of Perote for two years.

FELIX HOUSTON

A Mississippi planter, who raised a company of volunteers and came to Texas to aid in the Revolution shortly after the Battle of San Jacinto. He took command of the army after Rusk resigned, and when Albert Sidney Johnston was appointed to command, Felix fought a duel with him on the Navidad, in which Gen. Johnston was seriously wounded.

All the while Mexico planned the reconquest of Texas, but was so busy with internal revolutions that the Texas expedition had to be postponed.

We have seen how Santa Anna had in 1832 driven out President Bustamente, who in 1830 had driven out President Guerro, who in 1828 had driven out President Pedraza; and how he had made himself President before he came to Texas and San Jacinto.

In the autumn of 1836 President Houston liberated him on condition he would go to Washington and visit President Jackson and admit that Texas should be free. Here was a fine drama in which the protege of General Jackson, now the head of a nation largely his own creation, sent the captive Mexican Dictator across the country, a kind of message-bearer.

This obligation discharged, Santa Anna and his friend Almonte, who had shared his misfortunes, were sent home on a United States man of war. On a day in February, 1837, as they stood on the deck of the Pioneer and it approached Vera Cruz, El Presidente saw the towering peak of Orizaba, at whose base lay the Prison of Perote, the first glimpse of his native land since he had crossed the Rio Grande at Laredo in February a year ago.

Much had happened in this twelve months. Another President sat in Chapultepec, and Santa Anna, with the sympathy rather than censure of his countrymen, retired to his plantation and waited developments. There could be no peace in Mexico while this arch schemer lived, and he was soon at his old tactics. Bustamente was President again, and Santa Anna drove him out again.

And so it happened during the entire ten years of the Republic of Texas, that he was either in power, fighting to retain it, or out of power, fighting to regain it; and there was no time for Texas.

But a strange thing had happened in the United States. Ever since the Adams-DeOnis Treaty in 1819, when the States recognized that Texas was not part of the Louisiana purchase, and that it lay west of our borders, those in power at Washington had coveted it, and two Presidents had tried to buy it from Mexico. Gen. Jackson, whose term expired in March, 1837, craved Texas, and spent the last ten years of his life scheming for its annexation.

[126]

During Houston's second term a company of Texans under Capt. Fisher invaded Mexico in retaliation for Mexican raids on San Antonio. They were captured at Mier and started on their way to Mexico City. Four days march below Saltillo, rushing the guards, they escaped, but were retaken. One hundred and sixty beans were put in a jar, 17 black, the remainder white, and all were made to draw. Those drawing black beans were shot at twilight on March 25, 1842. James L. Shephard, one of the victims, was but slightly wounded, and lay like dead until nightfall, when he escaped and almost reached the Rio Grande, but was recaptured and taken back to Saltillo and shot.

The people of Texas desired it, and at their first election in September, 1836, voted all but unanimously for it. President Houston, whose fond dream was to return to Washington with a nation in his arms, sent William H. Wharton, of Brazoria, as first minister to Washington. He belonged to the Tennessee dynasty so powerful in that day.

Some of the survivors of the Mier death lottery had their pictures taken, and Freeman W. Douglas, of Brazoria, on the extreme right, brought it home with him. His granddaughter, Mrs. Ramsey, of Houston permitted me to copy it for my "History of the Republic" in 1928. The tall man, third from the left, was H. Journie (Journay) of Matagorda. His son, a very old man, lived on Smith Street here in Houston twenty-five years ago, and recognized his father in the group.

WM. H. WHARTON

First Minister from the Republic of Texas to Washington. Drank a midnight toast on the last hour of Jackson's administration with him and William M. Gwin, to the new nation.

But before he got to Washington he saw strange signs of opposition and wrote Austin, Secretary of State for Texas, with whom he had toured the States six months before in behalf of the Texas cause, "Somebody has been here since we've been gone." He heard the rumble, and then the roar of opposition and partisan politics.

The tumult and shouting for the victory of San Jacinto in April had died down in November, and where Wharton had been met by enthusiastic crowds of Texas sympathizers nine months before, he heard whispers that Texas was but a land of Filibusterers.

The lines between the Democratic and Whig parties were tightly drawn, and then, as now, principle must bow to party expediency. And while Wharton came with an empire, on a silver tray as it were, to bestow on the United States, he met the frown of the Secretary of State. Jackson's term was expiring, and in a few months he would be succeeded by a little Dutch politician named Van Buren, who feared abolition wrath. The great Whig leader, Henry Clay, who, as Secretary of State for John Quincy Adams ten years before, had with Adams' direction, tried to buy Texas from Mexico, now doubted the wisdom of taking it as a gift.

The result was that instead of receiving Texas with open arms, they would not receive it at all, and it was only through a ruse that the Senate unwittingly acknowledged its independence. In the last hours of the session a rider was attached to the appropriation bill, which permitted the expense of a charge' d'affaires to Texas when the President saw fit to send one.

Van Buren would be President in less than twenty-four hours, and those allowing the item to pass with this harmless provision knew he would not "see fit." Wharton rushed the bill to Jackson, and just before midnight of his last day the outgoing President "saw fit," and named a representative, which, under the clever wording of the rider, was a back-handed recognition. And down at the White House when the clock was striking the hour, these Tennessee friends, joined by William M. Gwin, drank a toast to Texas, and Jackson said to Wharton, "Let Texas claim to the Pacific," and Gwin heard this.

But the door was closed on admission to the Union for ten long years, during which time neither Democrats nor Whigs would espouse the dead dangerous issue.

[130]

Van Buren passed after four years, and General Harrison, the Whig, father of the mysterious Dr. Harrison, succeeded him. John Tyler, a Virginia Democrat, was chosen Vice-President, and became President on Harrison's death in 1841. He was hated by the Democrats as an apostate, and by the Whigs as an interloper. He had no party expediency to hinder him, for he had no party. So in 1843, looking about for an issue of his own, he set his heart on the acquisition of Texas. In the meantime, Houston and the Texans had opened an open flirtation with England.

JOHN TYLER OF VIRGINIA

The tenth President of the United States. He was a Democrat, elected Vice-President on the Whig ticket. He succeeded President Harrison, who died in 1841. Tyler staked his political fortunes on the annexation of Texas and won Texas but lost the presidency. Mrs. William H. Wharton of Brazoria presented him with a silver pitcher which is kept in the Tyler family at Sherwood Forrest, Virginia, to this day.

[131]

Tyler worried with the matter with little succees at first, for the presidential campaign of 1844 was just ahead, and Van Buren, who was to be the Democratic candidate, and Clay, who was to be the Whig, had both declared against it "at this time."

When the Whig Convention met Clay was nominated, and Texas was not mentioned.

Van Buren, defeated for re-election in 1840, had held the Democratic party together and retained a leadership, which got for him enough instructed votes, largely from the South, to make his nomination reasonably sure. Thinking he had the South "sewed up,"

EDWARD BURLESON
In middle life.

he was careful not to antagonize the Eastern Democrats, who were opposed to Texas, he wrote his celebrated letter against annexation.

William M. Gwin, of Mississippi, was in Washington when this letter appeared, and at once started a movement to divert the instructed South from Van Buren's support, and when the Baltimore Convention met in June they adopted the two-thirds rule, deadlocked it, and defeated Van Buren, and named James K. Polk, of Tennessee, on a "Texas Platform."

Polk was elected, and in the last days of Tyler's term a bill for annexation was passed, which was ratified by an extra session of the

MRS. WILLIAM H. WHARTON

Daughter of Jared E. Groce, who came to Texas in 1824 with a hundred slaves and opened a plantation on the Brazos in what is now Waller County. She survived Wharton nearly 40 years.

[133]

9th and last Congress of Texas at Washington on the Brazos the following July.

Formal annexation, however, had to await the formation of a State Constitution, which must come before Congress, and the election of state officials, all of which was not accomplished until the following February, and on the 16th of that month, 1846, Anson Jones, President of Texas, hauled down the Texas flag and unfurled the Stars and Stripes on Capitol Hill at Austin, and declared, "The Republic of Texas is no more."

J. PINCKNEY HENDERSON

The first Governor of Texas. On a balmy day in February, 1846, Anson Jones, the last President of the Republic, standing on the steps of the old wooden Capitol Building at Austin, pronounced the benediction of the Republic, and stepped aside to make way for the handsome and gallant first Governor, James Pinckney Henderson, of San Augustine.

OUR WESTERN BOUNDARIES

The first Legislature of Texas chose Sam Houston and Thomas J. Rusk Senators, and in March they were in Washington to begin their terms.

March 30, 1846, was an auspicious day in the annals of the nation, and long before the Senate convened the galleries were filled with

THOS. JEFFERSON RUSK

Of Nacogdoches, U. S. Senator from Texas. At the height of his career he committed suicide in 1857.

[135]

eager interested people. If one were called on to choose the most brilliant period of that body, which was once rightfully called the greatest legislative tribunal on earth, he would easily name the mid-forties of the last century, when the South, conscious of an impending crisis, was sending her most gifted men.

Into that august body, where the fortunes of Texas had been debated with partisan ardor for more than a decade, strode Houston and Rusk, and as they advanced to the bar where Vice-President Dallas administered the oath, a hush fell on the gallery and hall, and all eyes were turned on Sam Houston, who was making his reappearance in Washington eighteen years after he had left the House to become Governor of Tennessee.

An observer of this extraordinary scene wrote:

"It was a proud day when the Senators from Texas took their seats. Greatest of all the Texans, came that wondrous man who stood by the side of the infant Republic leaning on his rifle and rocked her infancy in those far-off wilds. Yes, there he stood at the bar of the Senate, bringing in his arms—not like the triumphant generals of ancient Rome, the fine gold or precious stones of distant barbaric princes lashed to his victorious car, but a new and vast empire!

"There he stood, the tall and erect form of the careworn chieftan, his locks prematurely gray from the hardships of frontier life. His wounds were upon him, for he had bled in the service of two Republics."

How much more worth while had been these eighteen years than if he had remained in line and had been the 8th President of the United States! Jackson was gone, but another Tennesseean sat in his place, and it remained for James K. Polk, an imperialist of the old school, to do what Jackson had so fondly hoped to accomplish.

William M. Gwin, of Mississippi, was present at a midnight meeting with Jackson and Wharton ten years before, when the old warrior told Wharton that Texas should claim to the Pacific. He greeted Houston and Rusk when they arrived in Washington in March, 1846, and sat in the gallery while they stood before the Vice-President. Six months before Calhoun, then Secretary of State, had spread a map before Gwin, and pointed to San Francisco on the

Pacific, with the remark, "Young man, when we take California, this place will be the New York of the Pacific." Three years later Gwin left Mississippi forever, telling his friends that when he came East again it would be as United States Senator from California. He had taken Jackson and Calhoun in earnest, and reached the West Coast in 1849, before statehood, and before gold was discovered. Four years from the time he witnessed the advent of Houston and Rusk into the Senate, he was back in Washington, the Senior Senator from California, and took his seat with them.

DR. WM. M. GWIN

United States marshal of Mississippi, friend of Jackson, Houston and Rusk. He left Mississippi for California in 1849, telling his friends that when he returned East he would be United States Senator from the Golden State, and he was.

But all this was not done as simply as it sounds. The extension and retention of these boundaries cost much blood and treasure.

The beautiful and fruitful land between the Nueces and the Rio Grande has a history almost apart from that of the remainder of Texas. In fact, it was not part of Texas until after the Revolution of 1836, and little or no jurisdiction was exercised over it by Texas until after the Mexican war, 1848.

About twenty-five years after the missions were founded along the upper San Antonio River, and the one at La Bahia, the viceroy made a vigorous effort to occupy the country, and commissioned Don Jose Escandon to colonize it as part of the Mexican State of New Santander. In 1749 Don Jose sent an expedition of families to found a villa on the east bank of the Nueces at its mouth, near the site of Corpus Christi of today, which was to be named Vedoya.

But the Indians were so hostile the plan was abandoned, and Vedoya is only a city that might have been. Escandon's occupation never got beyond the Rio Grande, where towns were founded on the south bank of the river at Comargo, Reyonosa, and other places. From these towns, where small garrisons of soldiers were kept, there was an occasional excursion into the country between the Rio Grande and the Nueces for the next hundred years.

These river towns were the victims of frequent raids from the Comanches and other Indians from the North for a hundred years, and during this time the Indian was the master of the country between the Nueces and the Rio Grande.

After a long time proprietors in these river towns began to have ranches up in this country where they would keep, or try to keep, vacqueros to watch their herds, but the cowboys often lost not only their herds, but their heads.

As late as 1807 the country was described in a land grant: "The wilderness which exists above the Rio Grande to the limits of the province named Texas * * * a vast body of unappropriated land exposed to the hostility of barbarous nations of Indians."

When the Texas Colonies were established in the eighteen twenties, this "wilderness" was traversed now and then by traders, but no settlement of any kind was begun within it until after the Revolution in 1836. At that time Corpus Christi was a name only applied to an imaginary "port" at the mouth of the Nueces.

The Republic of Texas claimed the country after 1836, but it was a claim only. The real beginning of Corpus Christi and the occupancy of the wilderness began with the advent of an enterprising person named Henry L. Kinney, who came to the mouth of the Nueces in 1838 or 1839, and began a career full of romantic interest.

A fair illustration of the kind of people who infested this no-man's land between 1836 and the Mexican war may be found in the account of Mustang Gray, told in the reminiscences of John Linn. Mayberry Gray was a private soldier in Captain Hill's company at San Jacinto, and after the war lived down on the border where he plied the trade of outlawry. He because famous under the names Cow Boy Gray and Mustang Gray, and a doggerel poem was written about his exploits which was sung on the frontier. But he was a vile creature, as the following from "Juan" Linn's recollections will show.

In 1842 seven Mexicans came from Comargo to Refugio to visit the ranch of Ysido Benavides. One of them was a relative of Mrs. Benavides, and brought her a sum of money. They had some goods which they carried to trade for tobacco. Mustang and a gang of cut-throats with whom he traveled overtook them and accepted their hospitality for the evening meal around the campfire. After dinner they overpowered the Mexicans, tied and told them that they had a few moments for prayer, after which they were all shot and their chattels divided and their horses taken back to Victoria and sold. One of the Mexicans survived and came to Victoria, where he related the details. The assassins were well known, and came and went with no effort by the local authorities to punish them. Gray was in the Mexican war and the country was favored when he died at Comargo in 1847.

But these so-called Texans were not the only scourge of this border during these years. Though not as vile as Mustang and his men, the Comanche made his periodical raids, and the recital of one of them will tell the kind of visits he made.

In 1844 seventeen of these savages made the rounds and included Kinney's ranch, plundered it, and killed everybody in sight, and were off with their booty. Colonel Kinney came home a few hours later, and was soon on their trail with eleven men. When he overtook them on the prairie, both parties dismounted for a free fight, focusing each other at fifty yards. Santa Anna, the Indian chief, designed to draw the fire of the enemy, and ran along their line, covering himself with his rawhide shield. Everybody took a shot at him at close range, but the bullets did not pierce his shield. Before they could reload the Indians rushed them. Colonel Kinney mounted his horse, taking a young Mexican behind him, and made a dash to get away. The braves followed and drove their spears through the Mexican, one of them after piercing his body wounded Kinney. The Colonel, now fighting mad, drew his pistol and killed his chief antagonist. The battle was a draw, seven of the Indians were killed, and three of Kinney's men were dead, and all the others wounded.

The Mexicans were not to be outdone in this race for villainy, and contributed their full share to make the land hideous. The story of Captain Dimmit will show what kind of visitors they were. Before the Revolution he had a trading post upon La Vacca Bay. He joined the first company which went down to Goliad in October, 1835, and after it was captured he was captain in command until Fannin came the following March. After the war he moved his trading post across the Nueces, about fifteen miles down the coast from Kinney's ranch. These traders probably had little respect for the revenue laws of either Texas or Mexico, but this seems to have been a gentleman's viewpoint in those days.

One day in July, 1841, a gang of Mexican outlaw soldiers raided Captain Dimmit's place, took all his goods, killed those who interfered, and carried Dimmit along. When they got him to the border he was started off to the City of Mexico, and when they reached a little ranch a day's march below Saltillo poor Dimmit took poison.

One would have a hard choice to select the most undesirable class of the population which infested this valley country during these years. Speaking of this rivalry of the races in which Colonel Kinney lived in those days, he afterward said:

"When the Mexican came I treated him politely, especially if he had me in his power. When the American came I did the same,

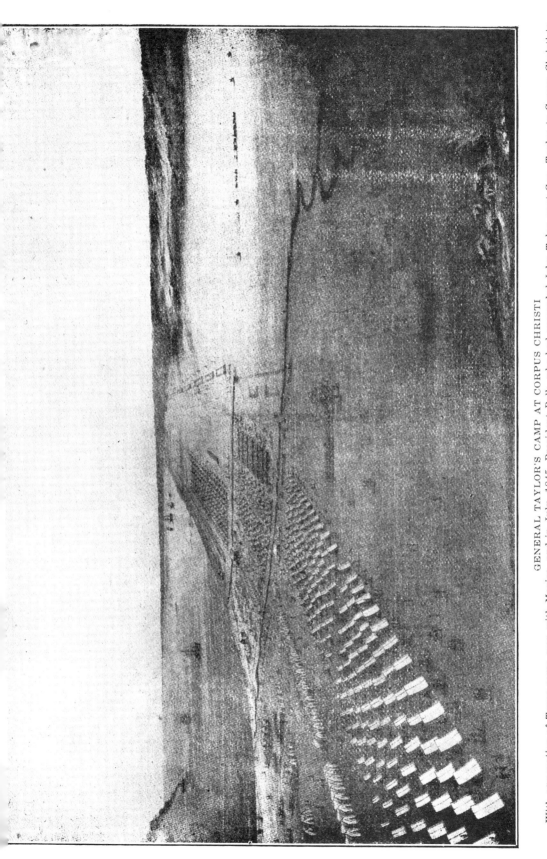

GENERAL TAYLOR'S CAMP AT CORPUS CHRISTI

With annexation of Texas came war with Mexico, and in July, 1845, President Polk, who had succeeded John Tyler, sent Gen. Taylor to Corpus Christi to be ready for emergencies. He camped on the beach below the bluff until the following March when, under further orders from President Polk, he was off to the Rio Grande, the Mexican war, and the presidency of the United States.

and when the Indian came I was often disposed to compromise with him."

But he fought them all alike when nothing but a fight would do them. While he was living in this state of perfect outlawry, things were happening in far-away Washington which determined the destiny of this boisterous border land.

Just as sundown on the last day of July, 1845, two companies of the Third Infantry of the U. S. Army, commanded by Colonel Ethan Allen Hitchcock, landed on the beach below Colonel Kinney's ranch. The entire regiment had landed on St. Joseph's Island, across the bay, two days before, and General Taylor had sent Colonel Hitchcock with Companies G and K on ahead to find Corpus Christi, to which place they had been ordered by President Polk.

They sailed on a lighter which drew four feet of water, and ran aground five miles out, where they remained two nights and a day. Natives from up and down the coast gathered about the lighter in their fishing boats, and on the second day the whole of Companies G and K embarked on these fishing boats, and at sundown were at Kinney's hospitable homestead, where Colonel Hitchcock noted: "Our arrival was hailed with satisfaction." Hitchcock was the lieutenant who carried Sam Houston's despatch announcing the victory at San Jacinto to Washington nine years before.

General Taylor waited reinforcements which were following, and further orders which came in due time.

Early in September Major Twiggs, with a regiment of dragoons, was coming overland from Jefferson Barracks via Austin and San Antonio. As they approached the Nueces a terrific storm was raging, and they could hear in the distance a roar like artillery. Bold Major Twiggs was sure that Ampudia's army was engaging General Taylor's little force. He rushed his reinforcements in battle array, and under whip and spur they came dashing into Kinney's ranch, charging a thunder storm!

President Polk coveted Texas and California, but he did not want war. Just how to divest Mexico of nearly a million square miles of her territory in a peaceful way puzzled him.

At this time Santa Anna was in exile, living in Havana, hoping for some turn of fortune which would enable him to get back home and to power again. He knew that a foreign war would give him a chance, but he saw little prospect of a war as long as General Taylor stayed at Kinney's ranch, and Ampudia on the Rio Grande. So he sent a messenger to Washington with a confidential hint to President Polk that he was not unfriendly to a boundary arrangement, and if Taylor were ordered to the Rio Grande and Admiral Connor's fleet should blockade Vera Cruz, things might be brought to a head.

These orders were given and Admiral Connor had a further order

CAPTAIN SAMUEL H. WALKER

With a small company of Texans, joined Taylor's army at Corpus Christi, fought through the Mexican war, was in most of the battles, and was killed in the very last skirmish at Haumantillo.

[143]

from the President, that if Santa Anna sought to land at Vera Cruz he should be permitted to do so. He came through the blockade and was again elevated to the presidency and the command of the army, and a year later met General Taylor at Buena Vista.

When Taylor's army moved down to the Rio Grande in March, 1846, it crossed the wilderness so long ruled by Mexican, Indian and American outlaws, the beautiful valley of today. The Indians,

COLONEL JACK HAYS

Came to Texas from Tennessee shortly after the Battle of San Jacinto, and went into the ranger service. He commanded a regiment in the Mexican war, where he won for himself and his Texans a national reputation. He met Gen. Franklin Pierce on the battle line, and when Pierce became President, he appointed Hays Surveyor General of California, where he lived for many years and became wealthy and a leading citizen, and founded the City of Oakland. John Hays Hammond, the well known mining engineer, is his nephew. The City of Oakland was founded on Col. Hays' ranch.

READING THE MEXICAN WAR NEWS AT THE COUNTRY STORE

Scanning the casualty list. Almost every village in the United States had boys on the battle front. The war was not popular among the anti-slavery folks, who saw in it a scheme to win new lands where slavery would exist. California, the first State to come into the Union out of the territory taken, was a free State.

[145]

awed by this show of force, had retired for the time, and the Mexicans and Americans living in this region had for the most part joined the armies of their respective countries.

Corporal U. S. Grant marched with the invading army, and in his memoirs written forty years later he said, "A more efficient army for its numbers and armament never fought a battle."

On the late afternoon of March 28 the American flag was unfurled on the north bank of the river in sight of Matamoros, while the band of the 8th Infantry played the Star Spangled Banner.

There were no settlements except scattered ranches along the north bank of the river, and Taylor's army camped in a corn field. The good-natured Mexican citizens lined the opposite bank of the river with curiosity, watching the invaders. Mexican girls exchanged greetings with the Yankee soldiers.

Almost daily for the first week there were desertions from our ranks, more than forty the first week, chiefly Irish enlisted men from the 8th Infantry. Now and then they would be caught in the act and would be shot amid stream, and in one instance the deserter had crossed over and was brought down by a musket shot from a sentinel in his own regiment; six or eight were drowned. The temptation of the Mexican maidens and the Catholic atmosphere was a great lure to these Irish lads.

Here, in speaking distance of each other, separated only by the river, the armies camped for a whole month, all the while each digging away at earth works, placing and removing and replacing artillery, piling bags of sand, each daring the other to start something.

Supplies for Taylor's army and recruits were arriving at Port Isabel, twenty-seven miles away, and there were constant rumors that the Mexicans would cross the river above and raid the supply depot, which they might easily have done. So, on the first day of May, a month after the flag had been unfurled as near Matamoros as one could reach without crossing the river, General Taylor decided to take his army back to Port Isabel to protect his supplies. Major Jacob Brown with the 7th Regiment of Infantry and an eighteen-pound battery were left to protect the flag and the sandpile fortifications in the corn field.

[146]

Ampudia and Arista, the Mexican commanders, took this strange retrograde movement as a retreat, as they may well have done, and pretended to think that General Taylor was running away to deprive them of the military glory of annihilating him. They issued loud manifestos as fast as they could be printed, and dapper Mexican dragoons dashed up and down distributing handbills.

In one they ordered General Taylor out of the country. In another they invited all of his soldiers to desert and join them. When they saw Taylor's column disappear in the chapparal their grief knew no bounds. "Oh, why did the cowardly North Americans not stand by their colors and fight? Taylor gave me his word he would fight and this is how an honorable gentleman keeps his word. Why does he fly like a coward to Post Isabel?" ran one of the handbills.

Nor did they stop at merely broadcasting this literature, but boldly crossed the river with six thousand men and placed themselves between Jacob Brown's corn field and Taylor's army at Port Isabel. And when the old "Rough and Ready," as his soldiers called him, was ready to start back to the relief of Jacob Brown the next day, he had to fight the two bloodiest battles ever fought on Texas soil to reach the corn field post. When, after a week's absence, he got back he found Maj. Brown had been killed and buried at the foot of the flagstaff. And they called the place Fort Brown, and the town which grew up Brownsville, even to this day.

Before leaving Matamoras after General Taylor, Arista and Ampudia had assured the people they would be back in short order and there would be a grand ball, and left the womenfolks to decorate the hall and be ready for a fandango of high degree. The night of May 9th and the day following were the wildest ever seen in the lower Rio Grande. In the late afternoon Ampudia, who escaped the field at Resaca La Palma and swam the river, dashed into the plaza at Matamoros, where the people were waiting in eager suspense, and rode around it again and again like a maniac.

The Mexican hospital service on the field was very primitive. When a man was wounded he was put in a sack and tied across a mule's back and started for the rear. All day the 9th and all through the night mule trains carrying sacks full of wounded and dying were plodding along to the river crossings. The roads were full of soldiers on foot and horseback, fleeing to Matamoros. At the crossing there were wild scenes of disorder, and the few leaky flat boats were in much demand. Hundreds piled on them and they would be swamped, spilling men and mules into the river. The poor wounded man tied in a sack had little chance when his mule was dumped into ten feet of water.

A young priest, seeing the wild disorder, got on the flat boat and stood with uplifted crucifix and demanded order. He was acting as a kind of traffic cop, and had gotten the boat laden, and was ready to shove off, when a panicky group of horsemen dashed up and rode onto the boat and upset it. Men, mules, horses, all were drowned, and when they found the priest's body the next day he still clasped the crucifix in his dead hands.

The war in Texas was over, and when Ampudia's broken army reached San Luis Potosi, Antonio Lopez de Santa Anna met him and took command.

Just before the close of the war Polk and his Secretary of State, Buchanan, marked a map to indicate the boundaries they would impose, and drew a line from the mouth of the Rio Grande due west to the Pacific. Later, however, it was decided that since this would include a population of two million in the Northern Mexican States it would be well to move the line and take in as far as possible only unsettled areas, and this was accordingly so done.

When the treaty of Guadalupe Hidalgo was signed in February, 1848, the boundary question between the United States and Mexico was settled, but the boundary question between the United States and Texas was unfinished business, which came near bringing on the war between the States ten years ahead of time. This great issue was settled in what has often been called the Compromise of 1850 (and the Omnibus Legislation), which witnessed the close of the career of Henry Clay.

As has already been noted, Spanish Texas was first the country east of the Trinity River, and later the name gradually extended westward to include the settlements on the San Antonio River. When the Spanish-Mexican state of New Santander was formed in 1746, the

Medina was fixed as its western boundary. Further up in the interior it was long debated during the eighteenth century whether the San Saba country was part of Texas, Coahuila or New Mexico. After a time the Nueces became the recognized western boundary of Colonial Texas, and so remained until the end of the Spanish and Mexican regimes.

The United States acquired Louisiana in 1803, and when Livingston, our envoy, concluded the purchase, he asked Talleyrand about the boundaries, and that wily person replied: "I do not know, you must take it as we got it (from Spain). Construe it in your own way. You have made a noble bargain, make the most of it." And Livingston wrote in his diary: "I san see the fate of Mexico."

Sixteen years later the United States and Spain ratified the Adams-DeOnis treaty, fixing the boundaries of the Western United States. They began at the mouth of the Sabine, thence up it to the 32nd degree latitude, thence due north to the Red River, thence up the Red River to the *100th meridian, longitude.* Thence *along the 100th Meridian* to the Arkansas River, thence up that river to its source, thence due north to the 42nd degree latitude, thence west along that line to the Southern Sea (Pacific) *as shown by Melish's Map.* This map, thoroughly identified, was attached to the treaty, and became the boundaries between the United States and New Spain (Mexico). When Mexico became an independent country in 1821, Texas was but an outlying Mexican province along the lower lines of this zigzag boundary.

When Santa Anna was a prisoner after the battle of San Jacinto, he was bargaining for his life. As the Chief Executive of Mexico, he negotiated with the Revolutionary Government of Texas the two treaties of Velasco. One was for public exhibition, and the other was a secret treaty, only to be exhibited after his return home, where he was "to prepare matters in the Cabinet of Mexico." When things were so "prepared," a treaty of limits was *to be* established in which the territory of Texas "was not to exceed beyond the Rio Grande." Santa Anna was to be returned at once so that he could go home and "prepare" for these things. But the Texans repudiated the pro-

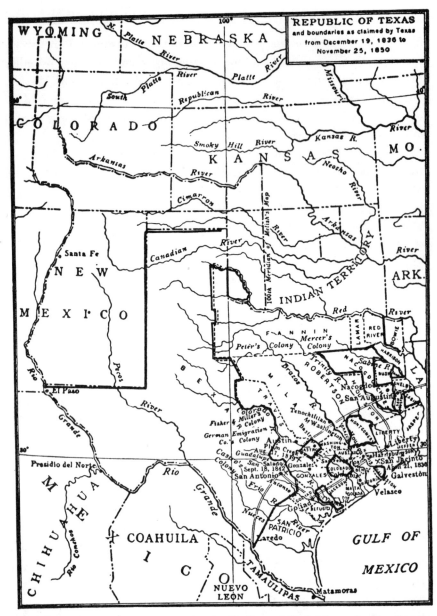

REPUBLIC OF TEXAS
and boundaries as claimed by Texas
from December 19, 1836 to
November 25, 1850

In the Treaty of Velasco, negotiated with General Santa Anna shortly after the Battle of San Jacinto, the Rio Grande was in effect fixed as the boundary between Texas and Mexico, but Mexico owned all the country west and south of the Louisiana Purchase, and the first Congress of Texas, in December, 1836, defined the limits of the Republic as shown on this map. They follow the Rio Grande to its source, in what is now Colorado, thence due north to the DeOnis-Adams line between the Louisiana Purchase and Spanish territory on the 42nd degree latitude, in what is now Wyoming, and follow that line east and south to the mouth of the Sabine, as shown by the celebrated Melish map, which is named in the DeOnis Treaty. Melish misplaced the 100th Meridian, and this caused the loss of Greer County to Texas.

When Texas entered the Union in 1846 it claimed these boundaries until 1850, when it relinquished all territory outside its prsent limits for ten million dollars, which went to pay the debts of the Republic. The territory thus released embraced about 65,000 square miles of the present State of New Mexico, 19,000 of Colorado, 4000 of Wyoming, 7700 of Kansas, and 5600 of Oklahoma.

visions of this secret treaty, and kept him a prisoner for many a weary month. When the first Texas Congress met in the autumn of 1836, it undertook to carry out this treaty regardless of its repudiation, and passed an ex parte act defining the boundaries of the Republic. They began at the mouth of the Rio Grande and followed it to its source (which was then unknown) and from this source due north to the 42nd parallel, which was the northern line in the Adams-DeOnis treaty. Then they graciously followed this Adams-DeOnis line, reversing its calls, east and south to the mouth of the Sabine, and along the north coast of the Gulf of Mexico, to the beginning point. This territory embraced in addition to our present territory about 65,000 square miles of New Mexico, including the town of Santa Fe; 19,000 of Colorado, 4000 of Wyoming, 7000 of Kansas, 5000 of Oklahoma, and it followed as one of its eastern limits the *100th Meridian*, longitude (as shown on the Melish Map).

During the next ten years there was intermittent war between Texas and Mexico, and neither country was able to hold a boundary. President Lamar made a gesture towards extending jurisdiction over these far places when he sent the expedition to Santa Fe in 1841.

When news of the fate of the Santa Fe Expedition reached Texas in January, 1842, the people were in a great rage, and to manifest it in a powerful way, the Texas Congress, then in session, had recourse to another ex parte act defining the boundaries of the Republic. They were extended by this legislative fiat south and west to include portions of the Mexican states of Tamaulipas, Coahuila, Durango, Sinola, all of Chihuahua, Sonora, New Mexico, the Californias, and all lands north to the 42nd parallel. President Houston vetoed the act, for though he was an imperialist of a high order, yet he regarded this as going too far, and due to the utter impossibility of its performance, he called it a joke.

But the Sixth Congress was in dead earnest, and repassed the boundary bill over his veto, and it became a law of the Republic. When the United States annexed Texas in 1846 it assumed the boundary quarrel with Mexico, and the limits of Texas were left for further discussion.

Anticipating this "further discussion," the Legislature of Texas in 1847, during the Mexican war, under inspiration from Ex-President Lamar, who was at the time a Captain of the United States troops at Laredo, created Starr, Webb, and Cameron Counties, all in the

MRS. PENELOPE JOHNSON WHARTON

Wife of General John A. Wharton of the Confederate Army, and their daughter, Kate. Mrs. Wharton was the daughter of David Johnson, antebellum Governor of South Carolina. They were the last survivors of this family, and are buried at the old Eagle Island Plantation in Brazoria County.

land west of the Nueces. In March, 1848, a few weeks after the Treaty of Guadalupe was signed, and before its terms had been published, Texas created Santa Fe County to extend north to the 42nd parallel, latitude. The new county, with Santa Fe as its county seat, contained over one hundred thousand square miles, and extended from the 30th parallel, at the junction of the Pecos and the Rio Grande, to the 42nd, now Wyoming, a distance of a thousand miles. It was designated as the Eleventh Judicial District of Texas, and Gov. Wood named Spruce M. Baird, an East Texas lawyer, judge, with instructions to proceed forthwith to Santa Fe and set up a county government. Judge Baird, armed with his forthwith commission, left Nacogdoches in May, going up the Mississippi River to St. Louis and down the Old Santa Fe Trail, and reached the county seat in November, but no one in Santa Fe would pay any attention to him.

During the next three years the controversy raged in and out of Congress, and the Governors of Texas, backed by the slavery expansionists of the South, loudly defied the United States until the Great Compromise Measure of 1850 was adopted. The Northern Senators and others opposed to slavery extension derided the claim of Texas to all this outlying territory, but Senator Clay said Texas made a plausible case. The Texans said if the Rio Grande is not the boundary now (1850), it was not the boundary when the United States Army, led by Gen. Taylor (who was now President) crossed the Nueces and claimed it in 1846.

Anyhow, the argument so far prevailed that Texas got ten million for a quit-claim, and our present limits were established. They fixed our north line at latitude 36°, 30′, the old Missouri Compromise line of 1820, our western, New Mexico boundary at longitude 103, from 36° 30′ down to the 32nd parallel (latitude), where it turned west along that parallel to the Rio Grande, to include a very small settlement at El Paso. Our northeastern line from 36°, 30′ south was fixed along the *100th Meridian* of blessed memory.

The age old quarrel now seemed forever settled, but not so. Efforts to locate the 100th Meridian on the ground showed a discrepancy between Mr. Melish's Map and the actual measurements. Then the question arose: which fork of the Red River did Adams and

DeOnis ascend to reach the 100th Meridian? If the north fork was the real Red River, then the land in the forks belonged to Texas, even if the meridian were moved west. Again the legislature was active as of old, and in 1860 organized Greer County in the forks of the river. The Civil war came on, and the 100th Meridian was forgotten, but afterwards the old quarrel flared again, and in 1896

ELISHA M. PEASE, FIFTH GOVERNOR OF TEXAS, 1853-57

Came from Connecticut before the Revolution, and was Secretary of the Ayuenta-miento at San Felipe. Afterwards practiced law at Brazoria, where he was a law partner with Col. John A. Wharton. Was a Union sympathizer during the war, and after the fall of the Confederacy was Governor under the Military (1867). He allied with Hamilton and the better element during the reconstruction days, and opposed Davis and his carpetbag regime. Pease was the first Governor to live in the mansion which was built with money gotten from the United States in the boundary settlement.

the controversy found its way to the Supreme Court of the United States. Texas claimed that the 100th Meridian must be fixed for boundary purposes where Melish had put it on his map. The United States claimed that the calls for the Melish Map must be disregarded and the true meridian found. Texas claimed that if the meridian must be moved 100 miles west, the line should follow it only to the north fork of the Red River, thence down *that* fork, leaving Greeer County west of the line and in Texas. The United States claimed that the south fork was the real Red River which Adams and DeOnis had in mind, and the true meridian when located must be followed across the north fork and to the south fork, and this would leave Greer County east of the meridian and in the Indian Territory. The United States won, and Texas was at last forced down within its present boundaries, which indeed seem ample.

THE LAST DAYS OF HOUSTON

In the twenty years since the Revolution there had been a constant stream of emigrants from everywhere, and in 1856 the population was over five hundred thousand. The old Baron's dream had long ago been realized. The Indian frontier was being pushed back year by year, and fully half of the people lived north of the old Spanish Trail, the frontier of Colonial Texas. The United States had established a line of forts from the Rio Grande to Red River, and the forts were being moved west as the frontier line was pushed back.

But more deadly to peace than the Indian menace was the gathering storm over slavery and secession. General Houston, serving his second term in the United States Senate, in constant contact with the extremists, North and South, saw signs of doom in the lowering clouds. He had spent the best years of his life to bring Texas into the Union, and as he declared in his debate over the Oregon boundary, "The Union is the guiding star of my life." Denouncing alike the hot heads, North and South, and seeing through the shallow demagogery of Douglass, he broke with his party leaders in 1855, thus destroying his chances for re-election for a third term in 1858.

The Democratic leaders in Texas and the Texas press followed for a while the sophistry of Douglass, and later the leadership of Toombs, Yancey and Jefferson Davis, and denounced Senator Houston as an apostate. In the conventions of over twenty counties held in Texas in 1855 he was denounced. Even Walker, his home county, joined in the clamor, and resolutions were adopted at Huntsville calling on him to resign. His answer to his critics was an announcement for Governor of Texas in 1857. The temper of the times is well shown in the result of the election in which Hardin Runnels, a Red River planter, beat him 9000 votes.

Two years later, undaunted by defeat, he renewed the contest and threw the full force of his powerful personality into his last campaign. Up and down the State he went denouncing the hot heads who would disrupt the Union, and predicting defeat for the South if the war should come. Limping on his San Jacinto wounds, he hurled defiance, and like one inspired, talked to the people he had served so long and so well. This appeal was too much for them, and he defeated Runnels by about 9000 votes, though at that time Texas was overwhelmingly for secession.

The very legislature chosen with him was against his views, and in derision of them he refused to go before a joint session and make his inaugural address, but made it to the world at large from the balcony of an Austin hotel.

A secession convention met in Austin, and on March 2, 1861, on Governor Houston's sixty-eighth birthday, and the twenty-fifth anniversary of Texas Independence, passed on an ordinance with-

This was probably the last picture of General Houston. It was painted by a Swedish artist shortly before he retired from the governorship in 1861.

These seven men cast the only votes against secession in the 1861 Convention. They were: Top row, your left, to right: A. P. Shuford, Jos. W. Throckmorton, Lemuel H. Williams, Joshua Johnson; bottom row: William H. Johnson, George W. Right, Thomas Proctor Hughes.

drawing Texas from the Union. On his forty-third birthday he sat as a delegate in the Colonial Convention at Washington on the Brazos and saw the Declaration of Independence adopted, and witnessed the birth of Texas as a nation.

He made his last swing about the country still talking in the same tones, and often angry people, mad with the passions of the hour, tried to break up his meetings. When he spoke at San Antonio, a Yankee army officer who was present wrote his father in Ohio, and describing the turbulent scene, said: "Of all men I have ever seen, Sam Houston comes nearest to the one who knows no fear."

The Secession Convention met and was organized by an assemblage of splendid Texans, who had determined to renounce his leadership forever, and go out of the Union with the other Southern States. They summoned Governor Houston to come before them, and he strode into the hall with a dignity and majesty rarely seen in mortal man. As he slowly walked the length of the hall there was a hush and respectful silence. As he turned his stern face upon them and calmly talked to them, they heard him, but heeded him not. They passed an ordinance requiring all State officials to take the oath to serve the Southern Confederacy. This he declined to do, and wrapping his blanket about his shoulders, walked out in old age and poverty to private life.

THE WAR BETWEEN THE STATES

Texas was now plunged headlong into a long and bloody war. In fact, all wars are bloody and terrible, but since the dawn of the race war has been man's chief occupation, and the age of universal peace on earth seems the dream of women and poets.

It was not a war against an alien tyrant, as our Revolution of 1775, and the Texas Revolution of 1836. It was war to the death between the States of our own Union. It was fought over slavery, over the right to hold the negro in bondage. The call which the Texas leaders signed for the Secession Convention in December, 1860, declared that the election of Lincoln threatened the "Domestic Institutions of the South," which meant the right to hold slaves.

In fact, the right of the Southern people to hold slaves *in the South* was not threatened. Mr. Lincoln pointed out in his letter to Alexander H. Stephens of Georgia in December, 1860, "Your property in your slaves will be as safe as in the days of Washington." But rather the direct cause of the war was over the right to take into and hold slaves in the territories that were becoming States. As Ben Wade expressed it: "The right to take a nameless nigger into a nameless land."

It has often been the cause of comment that a large majority of the soldiers who made up the Southern armies were men who never owned slaves. Why did they fight with so much vigor to protect the slaves of others? There were at least two interesting reasons for this. The Southern man who must make his living by labor did not relish the idea of competition with a million free negro laborers; then, too, there was a large class of Southern farmer folks who, though they had no slaves, hoped to acquire them.

A study of the resolutions passed by the various Democratic County Conventions in 1859, when they met to elect delegates to the State Convention, which met at Houston in that year, shows the temper of the times. In many frontier counties where there were very few slave holders the strongest resolutions were adopted for the protection of slavery, and for the elimination of restrictions on the slave trade, so that the traffic in and importation of slaves could be carried on freely and lawfully. The people wanted more and cheaper slaves, and a free slave market, and said so in these County Conven-

SOUTHERN WOMEN URGING UNWILLING MEN TO WAR

The women of the South, raised in the affluence of plantation life, were strong for secession and the Southern Confederacy, and urged their menfolks to the front to repel the Yankee invasion. Left alone with the slaves on the plantations, they carried on with great fortitude, and for a generation many of them stubbornly remained "unreconstructed rebels."

tions. Had it not been for General Houston's bitter denunciations, it is likely that the Democratic Convention at Houston would have advocated better slave markets for the people as various County Conventions had demanded.

But right or wrong, the Southern people were bent on protecting the "Domestic Institution," and went to war and down in defeat in an effort to do so.

The South had become an aristocracy of opulent land owners,

ALBERT SIDNEY JOHNSTON

The great Commander who was killed at Shiloh. After his duel with Felix Houston he commanded the Army of the Republic for a time, and was Secretary of War in the cabinet of Lamar. He lived on his plantation at China Grove in Brazoria County, which was his home, until the beginning of the war between the States.

which produced a generation of educated men for leadership, and from this class came most of our national legislators of the ante-bellum days, who were statesmen of a high order. From this class came the higher officers of the Southern armies, who made a most brilliant group of Generals. For military achievement and dashing and daring leadership, these men excelled the famous Marshals of Napoleon, and wrote the most stirring chapter in the martial history of the modern world. Lee and Longstreet, J. E. B. Stuart and Bed-

FRANCIS R. LUBBOCK, NINTH GOVERNOR, 1861-63

Began his career in Houston as a merchant in 1857. At the close of his first term he declined re-election, and entered the army. After the fall of Richmond he was with Judge Reagan and Jefferson Davis in their flight, and was captured with them in April in Northern Georgia. He survived the war nearly fifty years and served several terms as Treasurer of Texas.

[163]

ford Forrest, Stonewall Jackson, Albert Sidney Johnston, John A. Wharton, and many others rank high in the annals of war, and utterly eclipse the Northern Generals pitted against them.

The achievements of General Jackson were so remarkable, so spectacular, that often his name would bring shouts of applause from soldiers in the armies fighting him.

They were the kind of men who in all time have built empires; and had the South succeeded, as it came very near doing, they would have turned their legions to the South and the Confederacy would have seized all of North America down to Panama. Such plans were in serious contemplation, and had the sympathy of Northern leaders as well. Francis P. Blair, of Maryland, long in the confidence of Lincoln, proposed a truce between the armies, North and South, in 1864, and a joint invasion of Mexico to drive out Maximilian, after which, one wonders, *who would have driven them out.*

GENERAL E. KIRBY SMITH, OF FLORIDA

Commander of the Trans-Mississippi Department of the Confederacy, with headquarters at Shreveport. After the fall of Vicksburg the Federals held the Mississippi and the Confederacy was cut in twain, and Gen. Smith was for two years the supreme authority in these States west of the river. After the war he was instructor in mathematics at Sewanee University for nearly thirty years.

About this time William M. Gwin, Ex-Senator from California, conceived the idea of repeating in Northern Mexico what he had seen Houston and Austin do in Texas years before. He applied to Napoleon the Third, whose armies were then in Mexico, for a colonial grant in Sonora, with the purpose of filling it with broken soldiers and refugees from the South. Jackson, Houston and Rusk were gone, but this old Tennessean still lived and still had visions of empire.

The leaders of the South did not seem seriously to contemplate ultimate defeat. The story of Clinton Terry of Brazoria will well illustrate the confidence they had in victory. He was a lawyer, planter and slave owner, and a member of an illustrious family in Texas, a young man in his twenties. When the war was at its height, he wrote his will and counseled his executors in the case of his death to convert his lands and other valuables into money and purchase slaves as a safe investment for his family. Having sealed the document with these instructions, he rode away to die at Shiloh a month later. Recently I stood by the grave of this gallant young man at Sandy Point, and the lines of Tennyson, as he viewed the tomb of his crusader ancestor, came to me:

> "Gone the warrior, gone his glory,
> Gone the cause in which he died."

At first the military authorities of the Confederacy did not think the North would fight to hold the Southern States in the Union. Their right to secede was so clear that they could not visualize an armed resistance. So they discouraged the organization of troops from Texas, and our young men who were ambitious to fight had to enroll in regiments from the States east of the Mississippi. From the first, however, Texas did its part, and at the close of the first year, 1861, had twenty thousand men under arms.

An arsenal was established in Austin, where cannon were made from copper brought by wagon from Mexico. A cap and cartridge factory was established in the chamber of the Supreme Court. The State penitentiary at Huntsville manufactured each year over one and a half million yards of cotton cloth for the armies. For four long years Texas poured her resources and her men into the great conflict, and when on a day in April, 1865, the broken army of the great commander was surrendered at Appomattox, she lay prostrate and bleeding at the feet of the conqueror.

After the fall of Vicksburg in 1863, the Confederacy was cut in twain, and the Trans-Mississippi Department, which included Texas, was a military government of its own, and was the last to surrender, and a month after Gen. Lee surrendered the last armed conflict of the war was fought near the old battlefield of Palo Alto, on the Rio Grande, in Cameron County, Texas. Sheridan, the overlord of Texas and Louisiana, sent Yankee troops into Texas, and the first regiment arrived at Galveston in June. This was rapidly followed by military occupation, which lasted until the resumption of statehood in 1870.

THE CONQUERED BANNER

Furl that banner, for 'tis weary,
Round its staff, 'tis drooping, dreary,
Furl it, fold it, for 'tis best.
Furl it, for the hands that graspt it
And the hearts that fondly claspt it
Cold and dead are lying now;
Furl it softly, furl it slowly,
Treat it gently, treat it holy,
For it droops above the dead.
                    —*Father Ryan.*

RECONSTRUCTION

The darkest days of Texas were now ahead. The property-owning class, chiefly planters and slave holders, were ruined. Many of them were killed on the eastern battle fields, and those who came straggling home faced fallen fortunes.

Upon the death of Lincoln, Andrew Johnson, of Tennessee, became President, and his first utterances were rash and foreboding. "Traitors should be hanged," was his slogan, and every Southern man of any prominence thought this meant him. Thousands fled to Mexico to join Maximilian, among them Murrah, the timid weakling Governor of Texas.

ANDREW JOHNSON, SEVENTEENTH PRESIDENT OF THE UNITED STATES,

Succeeded Lincoln in April, 1865, and served nearly four years. His State, Tennessee, was in the Confederacy, but he, like Houston, was a Union man, and was driven out of the State. He was chosen Vice-President when Lincoln was elected for his second term and did his uttermost to protect the South from spoilsmen. The Radicals in Congress impeached him, but when tried by the U. S. Senate they lacked one vote of the necessary two-thirds for his removal. He named Andrew J. Hamilton first Provisional Governor of Texas in 1865.

[168]

But President Johnson's bark was worse than his bite, and he was soon at grips not with the Southern people, but with the Northern spoilsmen and job hunters, who came to be known as "carpetbaggers," who swarmed over the South with no visible equipment but a carpet-bag, inciting the negroes, oppressing the people.

Andrew Jackson Hamilton, formerly Attorney General of Texas, who had been a consistent Union man, was named Provisional Governor, and he made a valiant effort to rebuild the fallen fabric of

GENERAL GORDON GRANGER

The first Yankee troops to reach Texas after the fall of the Confederacy were 1800 under Gen. Granger, who landed in Galveston on June 19, 1865. The same day he published a proclamation that the negroes were free, and colored people celebrate June 19th to this day. Gen. Granger was a graduate of West Point, fought through the Mexican and Civil wars, and died in Santa Fe in 1876.

State government. A convention was called to reform the State Constitution to meet the new and changed conditions, and it is known as the Constitution of 1866.

"The Domestic Institution," which we went to war to save, was gone, and with it one hundred and fifty thousand negroes were freed and turned loose to wander almost like cattle. In 1859 there were more than 140,000 negroes in Texas, and their assessed valuation was nearly eighty-four million dollars. During the war thousands of slaves were brought into Texas from States east of the Mississippi for safety from the Northern armies. The same year, 1859, all the land in Texas was assessed at about eighty-two million, and all livestock at about twenty-five million. The losses of the war were terrible, and when you add to this a property loss equal in taxable value to all the land and more than three times the livestock of the State, it is easy to see the economic situation which faced the people.

The negro was now a citizen, with the right to vote, but of course without any qualification for citizenship. When let alone by agitators for the most part they were law-abiding and industrious. Gen. Gordon told a congressional committee in 1871: "The negroes have behaved so well in Georgia that the remark is not uncommon that no other race on earth suddenly relieved from servitude would have done so well." But the carpetbaggers so aroused them throughout the South that it took the grotesque performances of the old Ku Klux Klan to protect the white people from their excesses.

The great question of the hour was the negro, who was now free, and for whom the North was demanding citizenship and that he be put on equality, if not above, the white people of the South. During the war, while the masters were away fighting to keep them in bondage, the negroes had worked the plantations and faithfully served and protected the defenseless families with a devotion which has been the theme of song and story for many a year.

Speaking of their fidelity, General John B. Gordon, testifying before a congressional committee in 1871, said:

"When the entire male white population was at war and large plantations were left to be managed by women and children, not a single life was taken, not a single insurrection occurred, and that too at a time when the Federal Armies were marching through the country with freedom for the negroes written on their banners. The negroes have behaved so well in Georgia that the remark is not uncommon, that no race on earth suddenly relieved from servitude would have done so well."

After the registration was completed, an election was ordered to determine whether the people wanted a convention to form a new state constitution. For the first time in our history the negroes voted. Thirty seven thousand negroes voted in this election, all in favor of a convention and a new constitution, and under this sanction the constitution of 1869-70 was adopted. It was accepted by the Radicals in congress as sufficient, and Texas was re-admitted to the Union and a general election ordered to select state officials.

[171]

There was a cruel element in the South, then, as now, who would have oppressed the negroes, and there was a vicious element in the North, who not for love of the negro, but hatred for the white people here, would stir the black man to bad deeds. Under the inspiration of these itinerants, who raced up and down the land, the negroes often became vicious. They were told that at the first Christmas after freedom the lands in the South were to be divided, and each negro was to have forty acres and a mule.

GENERAL SHERIDAN

Under orders from Gen. Grant, who worked in harmony with the Radicals and defied President Johnson, Sheridan was put in command of the military district including Texas and Louisiana. He was reported as having said: "If I owned hell and Texas, I would rent out Texas and live in hell." A few years later, he having died, a young Episcopal clergyman in Mississippi named Kinsolving, said: "Since General Sheridan has made his choice, I will choose Texas." He came here and became the great bishop of his church for forty years.

The Convention of 1866 did not make the negro a citizen, but three years later, after the 15th Amendment to the Federal Constitution, our Constitution of 1869 did so.

Under the Constitution of 1866 James W. Throckmorton, who was one of the seven voting against secession in 1861, but who had been a Confederate soldier, was elected Governor. Similar procedure was

ANDREW J. HAMILTON, ELEVENTH GOVERNOR

A native of Alabama, practiced law at LaGrange before the war. Was Attorney-General of Texas and a member of Congress when the war began. He did his best to protect Texas from the Radicals. The *Houston Telegraph*, a leading Democratic paper published in 1869, paid him this high tribute: "Hamilton stood as a break-water between us and the floods of ruin. * * * He labored for a people whom he believed had wronged him, when the press of the State was heaping abuse on him, * * * and deserves the gratitude of all our people." These very people for whom he destroyed his political fortunes would have hanged him in 1861 had he not fled the State.

had in many of the other Southern States, and President Johnson hurried his plan for "readmission" of the fallen States. But this did not suit the spoilsmen who controlled Congress, thwarted and all but removed him, and took over the plans of reconstruction.

Grant was Commander in Chief of the Army, and though a great soldier was a weak man, very much of the type of Harding of our own day. He became the ally and tool of this venal gang, and it had its hands on the throat of the vanquished South.

The Confederate States were divided into military districts, and the egotistic despot Sheridan was put in charge of the district which included Texas. Throckmorton was removed from the governorship, and for nearly four years the State was ruled by military governors and our people suffered every kind of oppression and indignity.

After Throckmorton's removal the commandant appointed Ex-Governor Pease, who had been Governor, 1854-6, who served under

TAKING THE IRONCLAD OATH

As part of the Radical plan, registration boards were set up and the broken Confederate soldier was made to take the oath. Mitchell Thompson, a negro preacher at Corpus Christi, was a member of this board, and when an ex-Confederate soldier would come in Thompson would cut the buttons off his uniform. Ten years before Thompson was a runaway slave, and got near the Rio Grande, where he was caught and chained like a wild animal and dragged back to his master. The Radical plan was to disfranchise the whites and enfranchise the negro, and thus make the South safe for the carpetbagger.

military orders until he, like Hamilton, could no longer stand for the program in progress.

This program was to form a new Constitution which would disfranchise all those who had taken any part with the Confederacy, and enfranchise the negro, and make Texas safe for the Republican party and the carpetbaggers. But there was a respectable minority, like Hamilton and Pease, who had been for the Union, who fought against the radicals, and there was a fierce contest between these factions, while thousands of our best people could do nothing but look on.

The radicals were led by Edmund J. Davis, formerly of Corpus Christi, and he, with the carpetbagger officeholders, the negroes, and the aid of the military, faced Governor Hamilton, Governor Pease, and the better element who had the interest of the people of the State at heart.

In due time the new Constitution was framed, called the Constitution of 1869, and an election ordered. Davis and Hamilton were candidates for Governor, and if the national Republican machine and the Grant administration had kept its hands off Hamilton would have been chosen. But the spoilsmen and the carpetbagger ruled the party. There was a Gen. Jos. J. Reynolds, who was for the time ranking officer in the army of Texas, who had been a classmate with President Grant at West Point, and he controlled the election machinery. At the behest of the executive committee of the Republican party, Grant withdrew all Federal patronage from the Hamilton faction and only Davis men were chosen for office in Texas.

In spite of all of this, Hamilton was really elected, but Reynolds, who took charge of the returns, falsified them, and Davis was declared winner. Four years later, when Reynolds left Texas, he took the election returns with him and they were never officially filed.

The legislature elected along with Davis was thought to be "Simon pure," and General Reynolds, booted and spurred, wearing the uniform of a Major General in the Army of the United States, organized the 14th Legislature, which was under pressure from Davis and his henchmen to elect him to the United States Senate. When he had done all this General Reynolds rode back to his post in San

Antonio to await his election to the U. S. Senate. But the usurper was scarcely out of town when they forgot their bargain, and chose United States Senators from their own gang. Texas was now back in the Union, and Reynolds could no longer pester the civil authorities. They did not need him any longer.

It would merely prolong a sad, sordid story to tell more of the

U. S. GRANT, EIGHTEENTH PRESIDENT OF THE UNITED STATES

Though a great General, he was a sad failure as an executive. Tool of the Radicals, and a classmate of General Reynolds, who stole the governorship for Davis, we have no cause to revere the memory of Grant. He was also the tool of the Goulds and Fisks and the corrupt ring of politicians who disgraced the nation during his long term. The historian can only attribute his failures as a President to weakness rather than wickedness. For the soldiers who fought on a hundred battlefields, we have no bitterness. For the Radicals who oppressed and plundered a fallen people during the long night of reconstruction, we will ever cherish the bitterest memories.

doings of the carpetbag regime. Justice compels, however, a statement that though a vindictive tyrant and a tool of the radicals, Governor Davis was not a dishonest man. He had been a staunch Union-
ist, like Hamilton and Pease, and had fled the country to escape that
murderous gang called the Home Guard, which on the outbreak of
the war had terrorized and murdered the Union sympathizers. At one
time during the war when Davis was in Matamoros, he was kidnaped
by Confederate soldiers from Brownsville, and would have been
hanged but for the intervention of Mexican authorities. One of the
men taken with him was hanged. He had undergone much to pro-
voke him, but he was of an inferior type to Hamilton.

But the days of the radicals were numbered. The people of Texas
had gone to work to retrieve their fallen fortunes, and with character and courage they planned to redeem their State, and they did so.

In 1873 they elected Richard Coke Governor, and for thirty years
the State was controlled chiefly by the Ex-Confederate soldier, and
her Governors were either these soldiers or their sons.

CAPITALS OF TEXAS

When Governor Aguyo came to Texas in 1721 he crossed the Sabine and founded a presidio at Adeas, about ten miles from Natchitoches, and left a garrison of one hundred men and six cannon. This was the Spanish outpost on the French border, and for the next forty years and until Spain acquired Louisiana in 1762 was the seat of such government as Texas had. The Spanish Governors lived here, and one of them died here.

These Governors felt it their official duty to watch St. Denis, who remained the French commander of Natchitoches until his death in 1744, when the Spanish Governor Boreo wrote the viceroy from Adeas: "We can live easier in the future."

As soon as Spain took over Louisiana after the cession of 1762, the occupation of East Texas became less urgent and the outposts there were all but abandoned after 1772, when Spanish official headquarters were removed to San Antonio, which became the capital of the Province of Texas, and so remained until the revolution in 1836.

The first grant made by the Mexican nation in April, 1823, directed Austin to select a central location for a city to become his seat of government for his colony, and Governor Garcia took the liberty of suggesting a name for the proposed city, and christened it San Felipe de Austin, San Felipe being his patron saint. It was named before it was located. The first site discussed was on the Colorado, near where Columbus was later located, but Austin chose the Brazos as more central to his settlements.

From 1823 to 1836 it remained the seat of government of Austin's colonies, and was the most important town in the colonies. When Houston's army retreated from San Felipe in April, 1836, going up the river to Groce's, the town was burned to keep anything of value from falling into the hands of the Mexicans.

Santa Anna reached there while the fires were yet smouldering, and reported finding it in ashes. The government was more or less migratory during 1836.

[178]

The convention which declared independence and set up the provisional government met in March at Washington on the Brazos, but left there, going to Harrisburg and then to Galveston. Burnet's headquarters were for a while at Velasco and then at Columbia, where the first Congress met in October, 1836.

It was determined to select a temporary capital, with the thought that the permanent seat of government should be located later and further north than then existing settlements.

The two houses met in joint session on November 30, 1836, to select a seat of government until the year of 1840. The journal of this session recites that the following places were put in nomination: Houston on Buffalo Bayou, Matagorda, Washington, Velasco, Quintana, Nacogdoches, Hidalgo, Refugio, Fort Bend, Goliad, Groce's Retreat, Bexar, Columbia, San Patricio, Brazoria, Orozimbo. Upon the first ballot no place had a majority. Houston led with eleven

THE BUILDING AT WEST COLUMBIA WHERE THE FIRST CONGRESS OF THE
REPUBLIC MET IN OCTOBER, 1836

Here Houston was inaugurated president, and Austin, working in an exposed room with no fire, caught the cold which caused his death in December. The fate of Santa Anna was debated, and the first laws of the Republic passed here.

[179]

JA...S RA

THE TOWN OF HOUSTON,

SITUATED at the head of navigation, on the West bank of Buffalo Bayou, is now for the first time brought to public notice because, until now, the proprietors were not ready to offer it to the public, with the advantages of capital and improvements.

The town of Houston is located at a point on the river which must ever command the trade of the largest and richest portion of Texas. By reference to the map, it will be seen that the trade of San Jacinto, Spring Creek, New Kentucky and the Brazos, above and below Fort Bend, must necessarily come to this place, and will at this time warrant the employment of at least ONE MILLION DOLLARS of capital, and when the rich lands of this country shall be settled, a trade will flow to it, making it, beyond all doubt, the great interior commercial emporium of Texas.

The town of Houston is distant 15 miles from the Brazos river, 30 miles, a little North of East, from San Felippe, 60 miles from Washington, 40 miles from Lake Creek, 30 miles South West from New Kentucky, and 15 miles by water and 8 or 10 by land above Harrisburg. Tide water runs to this place and the lowest depth of water is about six feet. Vessels from New Orleans or New York can sail without obstacle to this place, and steamboats of the largest class can run down to Galveston Island in 8 or 10 hours, in all seasons of the year. It is but a few hours sail down the bay, where one may take an excursion of pleasure and enjoy the luxuries of fish, foul, oysters and sea bathing. Galveston harbor being the only one in which vessels drawing a large draft of water can navigate, must necessarily render the Island the great naval and commercial depot of the country.

The town of Houston must be the place where arms, amunitions and provisions for the government will be stored, because, situated in the very heart of the country, it combines security and the means of easy distribution, and a national armory will no doubt very soon be established at this point.

There is no place in Texas more healthy, having an abundance of excellent spring water, and enjoying the sea breeze in all its freshness. No place in Texas possesses so many advantages for building, having Pine, Ash, Cedar and Oak in inexhaustible quantities; also the tall and beautiful Magnolia grows in abundance. In the vicinity are fine quarries of stone.

Nature appears to have designated this place for the future seat of Government. It is handsome and beautifully elevated, salubrious and well watered, and now in the very heart or centre of population, and will be so for a length of time to come. It combines two important advantages: a communication with the coast and foreign countries, and with the different portions of the Republic. As the country shall improve, rail roads will become in use, and will be extended from this point to the Brazos, and up the same, also from this up to the head waters of San Jacinto, embracing that rich country, and in a few years the whole trade of the upper Brazos will make its way into Galveston Bay through this channel.

Preparations are now making to erect a water Saw Mill, and a large Public House for accommodation, will soon be opened. Steamboats now run in this river, and will in a short time commence running regularly to the Island.

The proprietors offer the lots for sale on moderate terms to those who desire to improve them, and invite the public to examine for themselves.

A. C. ALLEN, for
A. C. & J. K. ALLEN.

August 30, 1836.—6m
The Commercial Bulletin, of New Orleans, Mobile Advertiser, the Globe, at Washington, Morning Courier and New York Enquirer, New York Herald, and Louisville Public Advertiser are requested to make three insertions of this advertisement, and forward their bills to this office for payment.

PETER McGREAL,
in Brazoria, offers for sal...

FIRST ADVERTISEMENT OF HOUSTON

This appeared in the *Telegraph*, the only paper then published in Texas, on August 30, 1836, which day we celebrate as the birthday of the City. In December before a house had been finished, Houston was selected as the capital of the Republic until 1840.

votes, Matagorda second with eight, and Washington seven. On the fourth ballot Houston was chosen. On December 21st, the first session of the first Congress adjourned to meet in Houston on the following May.

"Houston on Buffalo Bayou," as it is written in the congressional record, was yet a city in prospect when it was selected on November 30th for the temporary capital of the Republic.

The Allens, who promoted it, had surveyed the site in August, 1836, and on August 30th had inserted an advertisement in the Bordens' paper which spoke in florid terms of the site chosen upon which they proposed to build a city. They described the location, "The Town of Houston is fifteen miles from the Brazos River, thirty miles from San

CAPITOL AT HOUSTON, 1837-39

It stood where the Rice Hotel now stands. Before it was finished, the second session of the First Congress met here in May, 1837. Lamar was inaugurated second President here in 1838, and began an agitation to remove the capitol which succeeded in 1839. During Houston's second term, 1842, on account of Mexican and Indian raids, he called the Sixth Congress to meet here.

Felipe, forty miles from Lake Creek, thirty miles southwest from New Kentucky, and fifteen miles by water above Harrisburg. Preparations are being made to erect a sawmill and a large public house."

As soon as it was chosen the seat of government, interest in it was manifest. Ex-Governor Lubbock, in his memoirs published in 1900, tells of his advent here about January 1, 1837. He came on the steamboat "Laura," which he declarees was the first boat that ever reached her landing. "Just before reaching our destination a party of us left the steamboat and took a yawl and went ahead to hunt the city. We found no evidence of a landing, and passed the site and ran up into White Oak Bayou, and got stuck in the brush. We then backed down the bayou, and found that we had gone past the city, and a close observation disclosed a road or street laid off to the water's edge.

"Upon landing we found stakes and footprints. A few tents were located not far away, one large one was used for a saloon. Logs were being hauled from the forest for the erection of a hotel where the Hutchins house now stands." (Now site of Southern Pacific Building.)

The Allens had undertaken to provide a capitol building, and on April 16, 1837, they began its construction so as to have it ready for the session of Congres, which was to and did convene on May 5th following. This structure stood at the intersection of Main and Texas, where the Rice Hotel now stands. And here at the appointed time, 12 o'clock noon, May 5, 1837, the second session of the first Congress of the Republic met. The indomitable Bordens, with their newspaper, followed the government from Columbia, but were a wee bit late, and in the first issue of their paper published in Houston on the 2nd of May, 1837, they apologized for the delay. "We left Columbia on the steamboat 'Yellowstone' on April 16, but were delayed a week by the surf on the bar at Velasco. We were then stranded at Clopper's Bar for a day, and reached Lynchburg on the 26th, whence we proceeded at the rate of one mile an hour to the head of navigation at Houston on Buffalo Bayou." When Congress convened in Houston on May 5th, Robert J. Walker, United States Senator from Mississippi, was a guest of the houses. During the

[182]

next decade he was the stalwart friend of Texas, and one of the most powerful factors in bringing about annexation.

While the resolution which fixed the seat of government at Houston provided that it should remain the capital until 1840, yet the location of the permanent capital was an everpresent interesting question.

By common consent it was agreed that the name of the city should be Austin, and almost the same consensus of opinion decided in advance that it should be located as far north as the old King's Highway, and on either the Brazos or the Colorado.

Though at the time there were few settlements in the dark and bloody ground north of the San Antonio Road, yet the frontier folks were pushing their perilous way into these wilds, and it was thought that the location of the seat of government there would make it a new center of settlement. The second Congress, which met at Houston in September, 1837, named a commission to "inquire into the propriety of selecting a site on which to locate permanently the seat of government of the Republic."

This committee was instructed to select such a site between the Trinity and Guadalupe not further south than Fort Bend or more than twenty miles north of the San Antonio Road. It made a report in November naming a number of places which it had considered, but without selecting one. No action was ever taken on this report, and in December, 1837, a second commission of five was named with instructions to examine various sites proposed, and make a report in the following April, 1838. This committee reported that it had selected John Eblin's league on the Colorado, adjoining the tract on which the town of LaGrange was located.

The second Congress, which was in session when this report was made, adopted it on April 17, 1838, and thus Eblin's league was chosen and Austin was to be located next door to LaGrange, in Fayette County.

Though President Houston had approved the resolution naming this commission in November, 1837, yet he vetoed the act of Congress naming Eblin's league as the site in April, 1838, giving the reason that since the capital was to remain at Houston until 1840, it was premature to select a new site in 1838, for any intervening Congress might at its will change it. It was generally thought that President Houston hoped the capital would remain at Houston.

There was a change in Presidents in 1838, and Maribeau B. Lamar and David G. Burnet became President and Vice-President.

The capital issue had been prominent in the campaign, and in January, 1839, Lamar approved a bill naming the third and last capital commission. The members of the commisssion chosen by Congress were A. C. Horton, I. W. Burton, William Menefee, Isaac Campbell and Louis P. Cooke.

The act creating it stipulated that the site should be between the Trinity and the Colorado and above the San Antonio Road. The committee first decided in favor of placing the city on the Colorado, and in April, 1839, reported "that we have selected the site of the Town of Waterloo, on the east bank of the Colorado." In their unanimous report they write: "The imagination of even the romantic

STATE CAPITOL BUILDING, AUSTIN

Under the inspiration of Lamar, who disliked Houston, the capitol was located at Austin in 1839. This buiding was constructed with money gotten from the United States in the boundary settlement of 1850. A stove was put in the Attorney-General's office and the pipe extended into an adjöining room full of combustible material, which caused a fire and destroyed it in 1881.

will not be disappointed on viewing the valley of the Colorado and the woodlands and prairies at a distance from it, and the citizen's bosom will swell with honest pride when standing at the portico of the capitol of his country he looks abroad upon a region worthy of being the home of the brave and free."

The Village of Waterloo was then the home of four frontier families, and was far in the Comanche country. In May, 1839, Edwin Waller, who had been chosen to survey and lay out the new city, was well under way with his work, and, guarded by rangers, the construction work began at once, and was so far advanced that the government, headed by the President and his cabinet, reached Austin October 17, 1839, and was received with much ceremony, which ended in a banquet which began at 3 P. M. and ended when the President arose at 8. Lamar was the chief factor in the removal from Houston prior to 1840, and tradition ascribes to him the selection of the beautiful site at the Village of Waterloo. In Volume 22 of the Quarterly published by the Texas Historical Association, A. W. Terrell, who was long identified with public life in Texas, contributes an article which dignifies this tradition and makes it a part of our written history. He says:

"Lamar, then Vice-President of the Republic, came with a party of hunters in the autumn of 1837, and camped at an old fort in Fort the Prairie, six miles below where Austin now stands.

"Jacob Harrell was then the only settler living at the present site of Austin, and no white man lived on the waters of the Colorado above him. His cabin and stockade, made of split logs, were built at the mouth of Shoal Creek, near the river ford. The hunters were awakened early in the morning by Jake Harrell's little son, who told them the prairie was full of buffalo. Lamar and his companions were soon in the saddle, and after a successful hunt were assembled by a recall from the bugler on the very hill where the capitol now stands. General Lamar sat on his horse and looked from the hill on the valley covered with wild rye; the mountains up the river, and the wonderful view to the south, and said to his companions, 'This should be the seat of future empire'."

When Lamar approved the act appointing the commission which

made the final location, he asked them to go to Jake Harrell's cabin and look carefully over the site, and they did.

It is an interesting coincidence that Austin, some years before, had chosen this site as a location for his permanent home, where he hoped to retire and live his latter days in peace, although this fact does not seem to have been known to the committee, which, after his death, chose it "to bear his name forever." There is yet in existence a letter which Austin wrote from Coahuila to Samuel M. Williams in May, 1832, giving Williams instructions for surveying for him

GEORGE T. WINSTON

First President of the University of Texas. The University was opened in 1883. The State has at various times granted it 2,500,000 acres of land, most of which it still owns. Great oil fields have been discovered on these lands.

what he characterizes as "the most attractive spot in all Texas." The location is to begin "at the upper line of the Tannehill League about five varas beyond the Big Springs at the foot of the mountain" (afterwards and now known as Mount Bonnel).

The survey was to include the "falls of the River."

He accompanied the letter with a sketch made from memory long after having visited this wild scene. "Here (he wrote) I shall fix my residence on the Colorado at the foot of the mountain to live."

His dream of retirement to this "most beautiful spot" was never fulfilled, but his spirit may have led the locators in 1839 when they went out into the wilderness to found the City of Austin.

The capital issue was not finally settled by the location at "Waterloo," but remained to vex the Republic until the adoption of the Constitution of the State in 1845.

Houston was inaugurated for his second term as President at Austin in December, 1841, when there was a salute fired by the Twin Sisters as the General and his party entered the village, followed by a great reception at the Eberly House.

THE WAR OF ARCHIVES

During Lamar's term the capital was removed from Houston to Austin, but, on account of Mexican and Indian raids, President Houston moved back to Houston in 1842, and in November moved again to Washington on the Brazos. When he sent for the archives, the citizens of Austin, led by the dashing Widow Eberly, made resistance, and kept the archives, which were deposited at the Eberly House for safe keeping.

Indian raids were so frequent that the people of Austin and the members of the government were not safe out of doors after sundown.

In March the following year a Mexican army under Vasquez raided San Antonio, and was only prevented from coming on to Austin by a rush of volunteers who rallied to repel the invaders.

The perils of the frontier and the further fact that General Houston had never looked with favor on the location at Austin, gave him an opportunity to remove the seat of government, and taking many of the government archives and his official family, he returned to Houston, where he convened a special session of the Sixth Congress in July, 1842, to determine whether an aggressive war should be begun against Mexico in return for the Vasquez raid. A bill for the invasion of Mexico was debated, passed, and vetoed at the Houston session.

Woll's raid on San Antonio in September gave a further argument against the return of the itinerant government to Austin, though the frontier folks were loud in denouncing their desertion.

To half-way meet the opposition, the President moved again, and in November called Congress to convene at Washington on the Brazos, where the lofts over two saloons were provided as halls for the houses.

The records of the Land Office remained at Austin, and the President sent messengers to arrange for their removal, but irate citizens voiced their contempt by shaving the manes and tails of the messengers' horses.

In December a force of thirty men was sent to bring away these archives, and loaded them on wagons, and when about to depart. they were fired on by angry townspeople, encouraged, aided and abetted by the proprietress of the Eberly House.

The company with the Land Office records loaded in wagons hurried out of town, but were overtaken on Brushy Creek, eighteen miles out, and surrounded by a superior force, compelled to return the records to Austin, where they were lodged in the Eberly House for safe keeping.

The return of the government to Austin or its permanent seat at Washington was a loud issue during Houston's term, and an issue in the election of 1844 between Edward Burleson and Anson Jones.

When the latter was elected, he continued to hold forth at Old Washington, and it was here in 1845 he received the diplomatic agents of the United States, England and France who came to parley with him over annexation. Here he called the extra session of the Ninth and last Congress of the Republic in June, and from here he issued the call for the Annexation Convention to meet at Austin on July 4, 1845.

It was this convention held at Austin which formulated our first State Constitution, and in that document Austin was named as the capital until 1850, when the question of a permanent location was to be submitted to a popular vote.

This referendum was held in March of that year, when Austin was named as the capital until 1870 by a vote of 7674, over Palestine 1854, and Tehuacana 1143. The contest in 1870 was between Austin and Houston.

SAN ANTONIO IN 1870
The oldest city in Texas.

There were churches here, a village, and a civil government, before George Washington was born. Here for many years the Spanish Governors of Texas resided. Here Moses Austin came to present his petition to Governor Martinez in 1820, Ben Milam was killed in December, 1835, the Alamo was stormed March 6, 1836.

One of the strongest arguments against Houston was the danger of yellow fever. A. W. Terrell of Austin wrote a campaign rhyme which opened with this stanza:

"Weary of toil, I laid me down
    To spend the night in Houston town and courted sleep
Lulled by the swamp frog's muffled drum
    And sharp mosquito's droning hum to slumber deep."

He tells in twenty stanzas of lively doggerel of a deep dark scheme between Ashbel Smith and John T. Brady, whom he overheard on this sleepless night:

"We'll buy the negro vote and move
    The State House to the town we love,
        And anchor it at Houston."

HOUSTON IN 1870

Harris County, including Houston, had a population of 17,000 in 1870. Houston had a population of 300,000 in 1930, the second largest city in the South.

And how they, being immune from yellow fever, will see it take off their enemies:

> "The Davis crew with all their sins
> And impious scoffings
> Before another year has passed,
> At Yellow Jack's imperious blast
> Must hunt their coffins."

Whether it was the yellow fever scare or Judge Terrell's doggerel, or both, which defeated Houston, Austin got fifty-three thousand votes against Houston's thirty-three, and the capital remains on the hill where Lamar had his early morning buffalo hunt in the autumn of 1837, and will remain at this beautiful site for all time.

The Constitution of 1876 set aside three million acres of land to be sold for the erection of a new capitol building, and with it the present structure was built.

CAPITOL TODAY

THE OLD CATTLE TRAILS

In the ante-bellum days the Southern cotton planter was the aristocrat of the land, and the old plantation with its slaves and prodigal abundance gave a life full of romantic interest to an era that passed forever with the fall of the Southern Confederacy. The slaves were now free, and the planters were for the most part bankrupt. The opulent herdsman, cattle king, cattle baron as he came to be called, was a product of the new era made by conditions which followed the war. Probably no phase of American life has held as much interest for the world at large as the epoch of the cattleman and the cowboy, fast becoming a tradition, yet today they furnish a large theme for current literature. The short story writer, the novelist, and the screen are very largely devoted to Western life, stories of the times of the big herds, and frontier characters, and the whole is gilded with a romance that appeals to the imagination and holds the interest of succeeding generations. The vast plains of South and Southwest Texas swarmed with millions of cattle at the close of the war, when unattended herds ran wild, on ample ranges in the equable climate that had been the winter grazing ground of the buffalo for untold ages.

Although the cattle industry had been a more or less thriving one since Austin's colonists first came, it had never had the advantage of ample markets, and the easy supply always overran the limited demand. In the days of the Republic drovers had begun to take herds east to Mississippi River points, and sometimes up the river. After the Mexican war and the gold discovery in California, hardy herdsmen from west of the Brazos began driving all the way to California, where cattle caught on the Texas ranges would sell for a hundred dollars per head. Many herds went overland to California before the Civil war.

But the California trails were closed by the war, and while it raged the cattle on the ranges of the Southwest multiplied.

[193]

At the close of the war there was a shortage of cattle in the North and East, and this was also true of the Western States, into which railways were being rapidly extended in the late 60's.

Just after the close of the war, slaughtering industries were opened at several places along the coast. One at Columbia on the Brazos did a big business for several years. Herds would be driven from all along the coast country, from as far west as Victoria, and from one hundred miles to the north, and slaughtered at Columbia for their hides and tallow, which were sent to market by sea. The bandit

COWBOYS

These rude looking fellows, who followed the herds up the old trails, have been made heroes of "Sweet Romance and Silver Rhyme" for many a year.

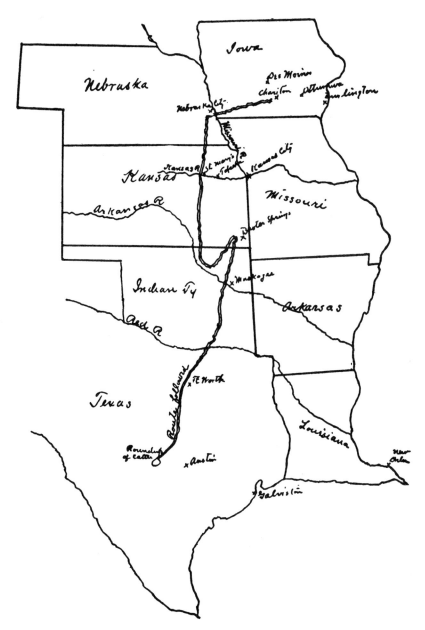

Map showing the route followed by George Duffield, who drove the first herd of Texas cattle north in 1866. This was prior to the opening of the Chisholm Trail. This herd was shipped from Burlington, Iowa, in November, 1866, to the Union Stock Yards in Chicago and were the first Texas cattle to reach that market.

[195]

Cortina resumed his cattle operations at Matamoras, and furnished foreign trade with cattle that he stole in Texas and delivered to boats in the mouth of the river.

In March, 1866, George C. Duffield, of Van Buren County, Iowa, came to Texas with the bold idea of buying and driving a herd of cattle all the way to Iowa. He went into the country west of Austin and purchased one thousand cattle at the substantial price of twelve dollars per head, and started with them on the long journey. Other drovers joined him, and before they had reached Red River they had several thousand. Leaving the San Saba in April, Duffield drove through Coryell County, crossed the Bosque at Meridian, then on through Johnson County, into Tarrant, crossing the Trinity in that county. In his log of this pioneer enterprise he mentions passing Elizabethtown, Denton, Pilot Point, and Sherman, and that he reached Red River on the 29th of May, six weeks after leaving the San Saba. He describes crossing over Red River:

"Swimming cattle is the order. We worked all day in the river and at dusk got the last beef over."

TEXAS HERDS ON THE NORTHERN TRAILS

From George Duffield's herd in 1866 until the last droves went north in 1895, an average of 350,000 cattle per year were driven to northern markets. Sometimes herds were driven as far as Montana and to Northern California.

He kept on through the Indian Territory, going towards Baxter Springs, in the southwestern portion of Kansas, crossing the Canadian just above the confluence of its north and south forks, and passing the present site of Muskogee, and going through Kansas and Nebraska, reached Burlington, Iowa, in October. A hundred head of the herd were sent to his ranch, and the remainder were shipped from Burlington by rail to Chicago. He accompanied the shipment and wrote in his diary:

"November 1st: Shipped cattle from Burlington to Chicago.

"November 2nd: Spent day at Union stock yard and in evening drove them to a slaughter house to have them packed."

This is probably the first consignment of Texas cattle that ever reached Chicago, and marks the beginning of a vast enterprise that has extended through the intervening years.

Duffield's diary is full of the most harrowing experiences. One reading it is impressed with the idea that he rode most of the way from San Saba to Burlington through rainstorms and across swollen streams, and that his herd stampeded almost every day. This diary

GALVESTON WATERFRONT, 1870

Trucks drove out into the bay and took freight from lighters, to which it had been transferred from ocean-going vessels.

[197]

was printed in the annals of Iowa by the Historical Society of that State in 1924, and is accompanied by a map which shows the way he went. He makes no mention of having followed any road or trail through Texas or the Indian Territory, and his trip evidently antedated the Chisholm Trail.

Jesse Chisholm was a half-breed Cherokee, who lived in the Indian Territory, and it is said that in 1866 he left his home on the little Arkansas River for a trading trip to the valleys of the Canadian and Washata Rivers in the Indian Territory; that he led his wagon train over the faint trace of the trail made four years before by the Federal troops under Colonel Emory, when they had withdrawn their posts in the Indian Territory under pressure from Confederate troops from Texas, and marched to Fort Leavenworth.

With a large train of ox teams, Chisholm went to Leavenworth and loaded up with Government supplies. On his return trip he bought 100 wild ponies and drove them ahead of his ox teams, and used them to settle the quicksand at the crossings of the Cimarron and the two forks of the Canadian. More than three thousand Indians with their thousands of ponies and the mounted soldiers followed the ruts of Jesse Chisholm's wagons and made a roadway which was christened the Chisholm Trail. Drovers from Texas would connect with this trail after they crossed Red River.

As early as 1867 or 1868 the trail that they made south of Red River and along the way that Duffield had gone had come to be known as the Chisholm Trail, although the half-breed Cherokee never drove a herd over it. In later years this trail was extended to San Antonio and on to the Rio Grande, and the name went with it.

Still other trails were opened crossing Red River to the west, and one at Red River Station between Belknap and Fort Sill, another at Doan's Store, above Vernon, and the general appellation of Chisholm Trail seems to have been given to all of them.

Emerson Hough, the novelist, who just before his death wrote "North of 36," one of the greatest cattle novels, lived in the same town in Iowa with the Duffields, and had George Duffield's diary before him, and was familiar with it, long before it was published.

Just at this time railway building was active in the Western

States. The Kansas and Pacific Railroad was extending to the West, but did not reach Denver until 1870, and as it went forward from one terminus to another, towns built along its way became the nearest shipping points to Texas. Each had its day—Abilene, Dodge City, Ellsworth, Cheyenne, and many other points. Beginning in 1867, and continuing actively until 1885, when nearer railroad facilities were extended into Western Texas, there was a continuous stream of Texas cattle moving north to the markets opened by this railroad transportation. Drives up these trails continued with considerable volume until as late as 1895.

In May, 1871, when Sherman and Marcy rode from Fort Richardson to Fort Sill, they passed large herds of cattle en route to Kansas, and on May 21st Marcy noted in his diary:

"Followed the old Belknap road, crossed Red River at Red River Station. This is the great crossing for the herds of cattle going from Texas to Kansas. The stock raisers in Texas keep an agent here who registers the cattle of different herds that cross the river into the Indian country. Each drover is required by law to keep a record of the number, brand, name of the vendor, and date of purchase of all the cattle he drives, the whole signed and acknowledged by the vendors. When the drover arrives at Red River he exhibits his purchase list to the agent, who verifies it by count and examination, and notes the result upon his tally register. This prevents drovers from taking off cattle that may have mixed with their herds and not been paid for."

The shortage of cattle in the West, North and East, and the fact that they could be sent to these markets through the railway connections in Kansas, furnished the first ample and dependable cattle market that had ever been opened to Texas. The prices paid were often very high, and great fortunes for those days were being rapidly made by enterprising persons who bought or otherwise acquired these herds in Southwest Texas and pushed them on across these trails into Kansas. The old Chisholm Trail that in the late 60's passed by Fort Worth, on just west of Decatur, and by Gainesville and on across Red River, was so beaten with the hoofs of passing herds that it was nearly a quarter of a mile wide, well worn beneath the surface of the surrounding prairie, and marked all the way by the bleaching bones of fallen cattle.

George W. Saunders, late President of the Trail Drivers Association of Texas, said in an address he delivered to that Association in 1916:

"In 1867 and 68, some of our most venturesome stockmen took a few small herds of cattle to New Orleans, Baxter Springs, Abilene, and other markets. The Northern drives proved fairly successful, although they experienced many hardships and dangers. The news of their success spread like wild fire, and the same and others tackled the trails in 1869. It was a question of finding a market for the stock at any price. There was very little money in the country, and no banks or trust companies to finance the drives. In 1869 drives proved successful which caused many others to join the trail drivers in 1870. By this time going up the trail was all the rage. 1879 was a banner year in all the markets. The drivers came home and began preparing for the '81 drives. Excitement ran high. There was never such activity in the stock business before in Texas. Thus opened the spring of 1871. Imagine all the ranchmen of the South, East and Middle Texas at work at the first sign of spring, gathering and delivering trail herds."

Summing up the results of nearly thirty years' activities, Mr. Saunders says:

"From 1885 the drives were lighter up to 1895, when the trails which had been used twenty-seven years were closed. Nothing like it and its far-reaching accomplishment ever happened before. It is estimated by the most conservative old-time trail drivers that an average of 350,000 cattle were driven up the trails from Texas each year for twenty-eight years, or a total of nearly ten million cattle, which represented to the ranchmen at home nearly one hundred million dollars. That a million horse stock were sold in the same way for as much as ten million dollars. The circulation of the millions produced by the industry, passing directly into channels that were open to receive it, produced the prosperity that has been evident in Texas for so many years. The cowman, the merchant, the day laborer, profited thereby, and the vast volume of gold that flowed into these channels is absolutely incomprehensible."

During these years many estates, vast in that day, were built up by ranchers in Western Texas. Often these ranches would include areas larger than a Texas county. The country was sparsely settled, full of rough characters, and each ranch owner and trail driver was a law unto himself. As is usually the case, when men come to sit in final judgment upon their own rights, these so-called cattle barons often became arbitrary and overbearing, and they formed a great barrier against the homesteader. The settler with all his worldly goods in a wagon, with his family and children, moving into Texas to locate a home and build fences that would interfere with the cattle trails, was looked upon as an intolerable nuisance, and long years of strife ensued between the ranchman and the farmer, which only within our time ended in the capitulation of the big ranch. But if the ranchman despised the homesteader, he loathed the sheep man, and there were years of strife between those who tended flocks and those who drove herds. With the passing of the big ranch, and the closing of the old trails, this interesting epoch came to an end, but it still lives in song and story, in romance and upon the screen. Those who read with thrilling interest the stories of Zane Grey and Emerson Hough, or witness on the screen the valor of the knightly cowboy might be interested in a description of him that was printed in an Abilene, Kansas, paper in 1871.

"The Texas cattle herder is a character, the like of which can be found nowhere else on earth. Of course, he is unlearned and illiterate, with but few wants and meager ambition. His diet is principally navy plug and whiskey, and the occupation nearest to his heart is gambling. His dress consists of a flannel shirt with a handkerchief circling his neck, butternut pants and a pair of long boots in which are always the legs of his pants. His head is covered by a sombrero, which is a Mexican hat with a high crown and a rim of enormous dimensions. He generally wears a revolver on each side of his person which he will use with as little hesitation on a man as on a wild animal. Such a character is dangerous and desperate, and each one has generally killed his man. They drink, swear and fight, and life with them is a round of boisterous gayety and indulgence."

[201]

Probably the Kansas editor was extreme in his characterization, but the sentimental fiction writer and the modern screen, which pictures this rude specimen of the 70's as a knight errant or a gilded saint, are equally wide the mark. The old rancher and his cowboy were a hardy race of men who lived in the open, fought a hard life, and were no better or worse than other generations of pioneers under similar conditions.

The trail drivers of Texas have gathered together in a large volume the traditions of these days, and it is a thousand pages of hardy adventure, triumphs and disappointments, and an intimate glimpse of a life that has passed forever.

Fred Sutton, who went over the trail in '81, tells the following pathetic story, illustrative of that life:

"Bert Phelps joined us at the old Boot ranch. He was a mild mannered, blue-eyed boy of twenty-two, educated and refined, and seemingly out of place on the trail. He was seen one day reading a little pocket Bible, which he hurriedly put away and blushed like a school girl when he saw us looking at him. Though quite modest and retiring in disposition, he was soon a rank favorite with all except Bill Driscoll, who never missed a chance to make light of 'mamma's boy,' as he called him. Bert was warned once or twice to look out for Driscoll, as he was a bad and ugly-tempered man. One day Driscoll met him at the water hole and picked a quarrel, drew his gun, killed the lad, and rode away. On a gently sloping hill, overlooking the valley of Red River, we placed the mortal remains of poor Bert Phelps. In his pocket we found a little Bible on the flyleaf of which was written, 'From Mother to her boy.' Where he came from no one ever knew."

It is a long, long trail from George Duffield's first herd to the modern stockyards, but it is over this long trail that the cattle business has made its way.

> "Ah, what tales of joys and sorrows
> Could these silent trails relate,
> Tales of loss, of wrecked ambitions,
> Tales of hope and love and hate."
> —*Ranch Verse.*

The system of herds on free ranges which prevailed for a long time was doomed by the passing of the public domain into private ownership by the lease system for public lands adopted in the early 80's, and by the advent of the homesteader. But it had a further blow by the coming of the barbed wire fence, which was well on its way in the 80's. Wortham in his "History of Texas" tells an interesting incident about the introduction of the new-fangled fence. He says that in 1871 a young hardware salesman named John W. Gates reached San Antonio with his samples, but found no one who would believe that this little wire would hold a wild Texas steer. To prove his case, he fenced in one of the plazas of the city and filled it with cattle from the range and demonstrated that his fence would work. The millions of acres of lands granted railways were being forced on the market, and the State adopted a lease system for its school lands, so that the big pasture rapidly encroached on the open range. This was a blow to the class of cattle men who thrived without owning land and paying taxes. Free grass was going fast, and prejudice against the big pasture and in favor of open range became a political issue. Men ran for office on a free grass platform. Unable to legislate against the encroachments of a wire fence, the gentry who felt aggrieved at the loss of the ancient right of open range had recourse to fence-cutting. It was easy for an industrious person with a wire clipper to destroy miles of pasture fence in a single night. In North and West Central Texas these night operators did so much damage that in 1883 Governor Ireland called a special session of the legislature to deal with fence-cutting and regulate the question of roads through the big pastures. The result was a statute making fence-cutting a felony and requiring all public roads to be left open. Free grass and the fence-cutter both passed away, and in a time the big pasture succumbed to the economic demand for harvests instead of herds.

JAMES W. THROCKMORTON OF COLLIN COUNTY, TWELFTH GOVERNOR

When the people of Texas adopted the Constitution of 1866 and elected Throckmorton Governor, they felt that they could take their place in the Union and forget the woes of war. But the Radicals in Congress, through Grant and Sheridan, overrode them. Throckmorton was removed "as an impediment of reconstruction," and it proceeded under military control. Throckmorton, though an officer in the Confederate Army, was one of the seven who voted against secession in the Convention of 1861. The negroes were not allowed the vote under the Constitution of 1866, and Throckmorton defeated Pease by a vote of 49,000 to 12,000.

THE STORY OF A VANQUISHED RACE

For countless ages the Indians were masters of Texas. When the white man first came he was considered by the Red Brother as a superior person, but the Indian soon found that he was without the attributes of Diety, and long years of strife resulted in the elimination of the Red Man. We have built our homes, our cities in his hunting grounds. This is the story of the struggle he made in Texas against annihilation.

The history of the Spanish occupation of Texas is largely the story of relations with the various tribes of Indians who dwelt here when the white man came. The Spanish Indian policy manifested during the entire course of Texas occupation was one of ostensible benevolence and high purpose. The conversion and civilization of the natives was the avowed aim, and for this purpose missions were built and maintained long after it must have been manifest that they were a complete failure. Millions of pesos were spent in military establishments under a petty policy of small garrisons maintained at remote places, never large enough to do more than keep a watch on the movements of the tribes and furnish a kind of intelligence on the activities first of the French and then the English from across the Mississippi.

One is led to wonder at the Spaniards' benevolent purposes and kindly advances toward the Texas Indians after understanding the ruthless course of revolting cruelties that these same Spaniards manifested in dealing with the Indians in Mexico and Peru and elsewhere in South America.

The reasons for this difference in policy cannot be attributed to any change of heart on the part of these ruthless masters, but rather to the fact that they were dealing with a different situation. The Indians of Texas were a stronger and more war-like race than those south of the Rio Grande, and they had no gold or other possessions for plunder.

[205]

The hundred wild tribes found here could easily move from place to place, and, if harshly driven, would seek alliance with the French, and, later, with the English, and such an alliance would mean the end of the weak Spanish occupation north of the Rio Grande.

In other words, Spain had competition in dealing with these wild peoples, and had known no such restraint in Central and South America.

EDMUND J. DAVIS OF CORPUS CHRISTI, THIRTEENTH GOVERNOR

The election held under the Constitution of 1869 was a contest between Davis, backed by the national administration, the carpetbaggers in Texas who controlled the negro vote, and Hamilton, who had the support of the better element in the Republican party. The Democrats were not in the contest, but those who voted supported Hamilton. He was elected, but Gen. Reynolds manipulated the vote, and Davis was declared winner. When Reynolds left Texas some years later, he took the election returns with him.

At the beginning of the eighteenth century the Indians of Texas could be divided very generally into two great groups—the Apache and all others who were ancient enemies of and loosely allied against the Apache.

The Apache was a veritable Ishmael of the plains, for his hand was against every man, and every man's hand was against him. As

RICHARD COKE OF WACO, FOURTEENTH GOVERNOR, 1873

Davis' term under the Constitution of 1869 was four years, and in '73 he was defeated by Coke, the ablest man in Texas since the passing of Houston. After the result of the election was known, Davis and his adherents managed to bring on a court action in which they got a decision by the carpetbag Supreme Court that the statute under which election was held was not valid. Backed by this decision, Davis tried to hold on, and appealed to Grant for military protection. The President replied that if he thought the statute invalid, he should have raised the question sooner, and not after he had sought election under it and lost. He was forced out of office, and this was the end of the carpetbag regime in Texas.

far back as history reaches, these tribes were hostile to all other groups with which they come in contact.

THE APACHE.

The Spaniards first came in contact with the Apache along the frontiers of Coahuila and Chihuahua, in New Mexico, and later in Texas. This general name was applied to the group of tribes in the immense space reaching from about the Brazos River in Texas west for nearly six hundred leagues, and they called these tribes in Texas Apaches de Oriente (Eastern Apaches).

The word Apache probably comes from the Indian word Apachu, meaning enemy. When LaSalle's men were among the Indians in East Texas in 1687, they were urged to aid expeditions by these Indians against the Apache, and when the first Spaniards came and founded missions in 1690-1691 they found all of the tribes east of the Colorado allied against the Apache. As early as 1692 some of the soldiers left to guard the first mission joined these Indians in campaigns against the common enemy.

When the Marquis Aguayo led his expedition into Texas in 1722 he recommended and sought a friendy policy toward these savages, and, as he journeyed from San Antonio to East Texas, he erected crosses along the way, in order, as he said, "to exalt the cross in the midst of so much idolatry, and to leave signs of peace to the Apache Indians."

But the crosses and signs of peace had no appreciable effect, and immediately after Aguayo's return Captain Flores of the San Antonio presidio led the first military expedition which was ever taken by the Spaniards in Texas against these savages. They had committed depredations about Bexar and hastily retreated to their own country, and Flores traveled 130 leagues before he encountered them. Among the captives taken by Flores was an Apache woman whom he questioned through an interpreter. She said that the reason the Apaches were hostile to the Spaniards and stole their horses was because of the trade which the Apaches were carrying on with "other Spaniards" to the north, to whom they sold the horses and slaves.

These "other Spaniards" to the north were the French traders from Louisiana, who operated along Red River and maintained friendly relations with all the Indian tribes.

Dr. Bolton says that a rendezvous or trading station was maintained on Red River, near where the town of Ringgold now stands, where for many years the Apaches and Comanches and other tribes would bring horses they had stolen from San Antonio and along

RICHARD B. HUBBARD OF TYLER, FIFTEENTH GOVERNOR, 1876-78

When Governor Coke took his seat in the U. S. Senate he was succeeded by Lieutenant-Governor Hubbard. In the Democratic State Convention at Austin in July, 1878, there was a deadlock between Hubbard and Throckmorton for the gubernatorial nomination. After a week of balloting, the honor was offered Judge Reagan, who declined on account of his services in Congress. Roberts was nominated.

the Rio Grande, and sell them to the French. The French would also purchase from them for slaves captives taken in their wars with one another.

About 1700 the Comanches, coming from the Wyoming country, had reached North New Mexico and the Panhandle country of Texas and Kansas, driving the Apache from these regions, and from that time forward these tribes were deadly enemies and continually at war.

ORAN M. ROBERTS OF SAN AUGUSTINE, SIXTEENTH GOVERNOR, 1878-1882

Was chosen a Justice of the Supreme Court to succeed Judge Lipscomb in 1857. Resigned to lead a regiment in the Confederate Army. Was elected Chief Justice in the same court to succeed Judge Wheeler, who committed suicide in 1864. Chosen to the U. S. Senate in 1866, but was refused admission by the Radicals. Appointed Chief Justice in the Supreme Court again in 1876, which position he was holding when he was elected Governor in 1878.

The Apaches were pressed south towards the Rio Grande and nearer the Bexar settlements. The Comanches took up the trade with the French that the Apaches had carried on, and would rob the Apaches of their horses and carry away captive Apache Indians to be sold for slaves at the Red River rendezvous, and taken down the river to the plantations.

These formidable tribes, the Comanche and Apache, were chiefly the barriers that had resisted Spanish influences in Texas for centuries, and this was one of the many causes which led to the admission of Austin's colonies.

During the colonial period, 1821-1836, there was constant friction with various Indian tribes, but no vigorous invasion was ever undertaken by the Indians who held sway to the north of the old Spanish Trail.

At the time of the Revolution all of the Indian tribes were growing restless at the constant encroachment of white settlers, yet they had nothing in common with Mexico. We have seen how the Consultation made them fair promises in the autumn of 1835, and how General Houston went among them and made treaties which kept them quiet during the San Jacinto Campaign. But when it was over and the Mexicans driven out, the Republic repudiated its promises and trouble began. Mexican agents were now sent among them with fair promises that if they would help drive out the colonists, Mexico would give them their hunting grounds. The first strife was with the Cherokees.

THE PASSING OF THE CHEROKEES.

The Cherokees were perhaps the most enlightened of all the North American Indians. They had a highly developed tribal government, an alphabet, a kind of rude literature, and stern notions of individual property rights. Many of them were slave owners, and those who came to Texas in the early '20s were as well qualified for citizenship as the average Mexican of that period, who was himself an Indian of far less force than the Cherokee.

The story of the Cherokee expulsion has been best told by John H. Reagan, who was in the fight. Reagan, who was a youth of twenty-one at the time, went with Lacy, the Indian agent who was sent by President Lamar to notify the Cherokees that because of their repeated crimes against the whites and their continued intrigues with Mexican emissaries, they must leave Texas, and go back to the territory of the United States, from whence they had come twenty years before.

"When we reached the residence of Chief Bowles, he invited us to a fine spring near his house, where we were seated, and Lamar's

RICHARD FIELDS

Was the chief of the Cherokees in East Texas. He and John Dunn Hunter made an alliance with the Edwards at Nacogdoches in 1827, by which the Cherokees and the newly arrived settlers from the States were to take East Texas from Mexico and divide it between the Cherokees and the Fredonians, as Edwards' followers were called.

[212]

message was read to him. Bowles said he could not answer as to abandoning the country until he could consult with his people, and he was given ten days. We returned to his house at the expiration of this time, and he said his young men were for war, and thought they could whip the whites, but he knew that in the end the whites would

JOHN H. REAGAN

Was for fifty years a great leader in Texas, District Judge at Palestine, and a member of Congress before the war, Postmaster General in the cabinet of Jefferson Davis. After the war he returned to his farm and went to work. While plowing his field in 1867 Gen. Griffin, the Military Dictator of Texas, delivered him an offer of appointment as Provisional Governor of Texas. He declined, saying he would accept no office to which he was not elected by the people whom he served. He was the leading spirit in the formation of our last Constitution of 1876. Later he was United States Senator from Texas and Railroad Commissioner. He died in 1905, aged 87 years.

win. He said that while it was true that they never had a title from the Mexican Government, yet General Houston had confirmed their right to the country by treaty.

"He told of a plan he had on foot to join his tribe with the main body of the Cherokees in the States and take them all to California, and asked for time to gather their crops. (This was June, 1839.)

"Lacy told Bowles he had no authority to give him any such time. Bowles then said it mattered little to him, that he was now eighty-three years old and would not live much longer, but he felt a great interest in the future of his wives and children. That his tribe had always been true to him, and though he differed with them as to the course he pursued, yet they wanted war rather than go, and war it must be.

"The colonists had determined upon their immediate expulsion, and three regiments were approaching, one led by Rusk, another Landrum's Red Landers, and the third Edward Burleson's Regulars. While Rusk was waiting for the two other regiments to come up, Bowles was seeking delay so that warriors from other tribes might reach him, and Rusk and Bowles agreed upon a neutral line that was not to be crossed by either party without giving notice to the other. About sunrise on the morning of July 15th, John Bowles, a son of the Chief, and Fox Fields, son of Richard Fields, former Chief, rode to our camp and notified Albert Sidney Johnston that they were ready to move north across the neutral strip, and General Johnston thanked them and told them that the Texans would cross the Neches after them.

"There were battles on the next two days, in which the Indians fought with great valour. Chief Bowles remained on the field on horseback, wearing a handsome sword and sash which had been given him by President Houston. He was a magnificent picture of barbaric manhood, and was the last to leave the field when the Indians retreated. He was wounded and his horse disabled, and he dismounted, and as he walked away was shot in the back and fell. Then as he sat up with his face towards us, I started to him to secure his surrender.

"At the same instant my Captain, Bob Smith, ran towards him

with a drawn pistol, and we reached Bowles at the same instant. Realizing what was imminent, I called, 'Captain, don't shoot him,' but he fired, striking Bowles in the head, killing him instantly."

The Cherokees moved north, and were subsequently joined with scattered remnants of their once powerful tribe, and located in the "Cherokee Nation." Judge Reagan says that besides Cherokee warriors, there were Shawnees, Delawares, Kickapoos and Indians from various other small tribes then living in North and Northeast Texas engaged in this battle.

JOHN IRELAND OF SEGUIN, SEVENTEENTH GOVERNOR, 1882-1886

Practiced law at Seguin before the war. Entered the service as a private, and became Colonel. Justice of Supreme Court, 1875.

[215]

General Houston was very bitter in his opposition to this campaign, and it brought down his great wrath upon the Lamar administration; and ever afterwards he held an almost savage hatred for Albert Sidney Johnston, whom he regarded as a strong instrument in bringing it about.

THE COMANCHE.

Distinguished from the Cherokees and East Texas Indians, the many wild tribes who dwelt and roved further to the west were often referred to as the prairie Indians. There were a number of these tribes, but the most formidable of them was the Comanche. The Comanche roved up and down the vast West from the Kansas prairies to the Gulf of Mexico, often taking side trips or excursions down into Mexico, where he always left a bloody trail. He rarely came east of the Lower Brazos, but there is not a village or hamlet west of the Colorado from Port Lavaca to the Red River that is without a tradition of his midnight visit.

He would come South in the winter along with the buffalo, which he called his cattle, and would seek the higher, cooler climate of the plateaus in the summer.

They drove the Apache to and across the Rio Grande, and had become the terror of the Bexar settlements. From the time the first colonists came in 1821, they were the menace of the Northwestern frontier.

It was the custom of the Comanches after a raid into Mexico to stop by the way of San Antonio and trade, and often after excursions into Texas settlements they would boldly come into San Antonio and offer their captives for ransom. On such occasions they would ride up to the Commandant and require him to keep their horses and chattels while they went up town for a frolic. They made a kind of a groom out of the small command which was depended on for garrison by the helpless population.

Albert Sidney Johnston was in San Antonio on one occasion in 1839 when a band of warriors came to town, and relates an interesting incident:

Essowakkeny, the Comanche chief, dismounted, and pointing to his horses, said: "There is our caballado, take care of it." "Yes," said General Johnston, looking steadily at him; "you ride good horses; I take care of mine, you take care of yours." And the Indian met the fearless gaze of a warrior as bold as himself, and with a grim smile, detailed some of his own men to watch his horses.

In February, 1840, the Comanches agreed to bring all their white

A PRISONER AMONG THE COMANCHES

The Comanche battle line lay along the entire northwestern frontier, where for three-quartrs of a century he held back Spaniard and American, protecting his hunting ground to the last. He alternately fought the Apache, whom he drove from the plains, and the white man, whom he kept from these plains until long after the Civil war.

prisoners whom they were holding for ransom into San Antonio and deliver them to their families, and make a treaty with the Republic. Three commissioners were named by the government to meet the Comanche chiefs.

On March 19th, thirty-two warriors with their women and children came in for the pow-wow. Twelve chiefs met the three commissioners at the stone council house, and the talk was opened by the surrender of Colonel Lockhart's daughter, who had been captured at Gonzales the year before. Colonel Fisher, one of the commissioners, asked them where the other prisoners were, and they replied that she was the only one they had. The Lockhart girl then related that there were others in their camps whom they were holding back for larger ransoms.

Colonel Fisher told them of their wickedness, and demanded that they bring in the other prisoners, and named thirteen persons whom they were known to have captured within recent months. Turning full upon them, he said: "Do you remember murdering two men, and carrying away this girl (Miss Lockhart) when you were returning from Houston last year under a flag of truce?" There was a silence for a moment after this challenge, when one of the chiefs arose, and standing his full height, said, with haughty insolence, "No, we do not recollect," and sat down. There was another pause, and he arose again and defiantly said to Colonel Fisher: "How do you like our answer?" Colonel Fisher replied, "I do not like your answer. I told you not to come here without all your prisoners; your women and braves may depart in peace, but we will hold your chiefs as hostages until the other white captives are brought in."

At this moment Captain Howard marched in a company of fifty soldiers. Instantly the Indians strung their bows and gave the war whoop. One of them sprang upon Captain Howard, striking him down with a knife. In the interval of a few moments all the chiefs were slain. There were twenty warriors without the building, and when they heard the war whoop inside they all at once attacked the people, but all of them were killed save one, who escaped into a house. Wishing to spare him, they sent an Indian woman to tell him that they would allow him to leave the house unmolested if he would go peacefully. He defied them, and refused their permission, and stepped from the building with his bow strung and ready for combat.

Mrs. Samuel Mavrick, in her diary published many years after, related that she, with a crowd of bystanders, was watching some small Indian boys who had come in with the party do some clever target shooting at a tree on the river bank. When the war whoop sounded and before the onlookers realized what it meant one of these boys turned like a flash and shot an arrow into the crowd, striking a bystander in the heart. Mrs. Mavrick gathered her chil-

MAJOR LYSANDER WELLS

Second Regiment, San Jacinto. Was in the Council House fight. Was killed in a duel in San Antonio in 1840.

dren inside the enclosure about her house on Soledad Street and kept watch, and this is what she saw:

"An Indian was dying near my street door and a white man came up and pointed a pistol at him. I called out, 'Don't shoot, he is dying.' The man said, 'I was going to put him out of his misery, but to please you'—and he put up his pistol. Just then Lysander Wells rode by going up Soledad Street. He was mounted on a fine horse with a silver mounted saddle and bridle. As he reached the

In September, 1838, Walter P. Lane, with a party of surveyors, went into the Indian country in what is now Navarro County, and encountered a band of Kickapoos hunting. The Indians thinking the white men were hunters, welcomed them. But when they found they were surveyors they first plead with them to go back, and unable to dissuade them, killed 16 of Lane's men and wounded others. The wounded later fell in with other Kickapoos, who did not know they were surveyors, and who treated them kindly.

Vermandi House an Indian who had escaped detection rushed out from his hiding place, and jumping on the horse behind Wells, clasped his arms and tried to reach his bridle reins. The two men struggled for some time until Wells managed to draw his pistol, when he turned and placed it against the Indian's body and fired. The Indian released his grasp and fell dying. Wells put spurs to his horse and dashed away in pursuit of other Indians."

The so-called council house in which this gathering was held was the old Spanish Cabildo, in which Governor Martinez had received Moses Austin, which at the time was being used for a court house. Judge John Hemphill, then a District Judge of the Republic, was in San Antonio holding court, and it had adjourned for the council meeting with the Comanche chiefs. Judge Hemphill was in the hall, a mere onlooker, when the fight started. He was attacked by one of the braves and they fought with knives. Judge Hemphill killed his antagonist, and lived to be Chief Justice of the State of Texas and United States Senator from Texas.

Years of terrible, bloody warfare with the Comanches and their allied tribes followed this fateful day.

In the following August a thousand warriors from the Comanche country swept down the valley of the Guadalupe to Linnville, on Matagorda Bay, capturing and killing and plundering. As they started back with their booty, companies of Minute Men from most every colony west of the Colorado were on their trail, and nearly 300 well-armed frontiersmen under General Felix Houston fought with them in the battle of Plum Creek, near where Lockhart now stands, in which the raiders were routed.

FRONTIERS OF THE FIFTIES.

When annexation was accomplished, the people of Texas believed that their troubles were over; that they would have stability at home and protection against the Mexicans and Indians who had harassed them during the days of the Republic. The Mexican war, which immediately followed, when the Federal Government poured troups along the border and into Mexico, punished the Mexicans in a way that the Texans had long hoped to see.

In the beginning of the Mexican war the United States Government was confronted with the same situation that had confronted the colonists in 1836, when Santa Anna's invasion was imminent.

OVERLAND STAGE, PASSING THROUGH THE INDIAN COUNTRY

In 1857 Congress established a stage line from the Mississippi River to San Francisco, with termini at St. Louis and Memphis. It crossed the Red River into Texas at Preston, near Gainesville, and left Texas near El Paso. The trip from St. Louis to Frisco was sometimes made in 25 days. Through most of Texas the stage had a military escort to protect it from the Indians. The line from El Paso crossed the headwaters of the Concho, passed Fort Shadburn, Phantom Hill, Belknap, Jacksboro, Bridgeport, Gainesville.

If the Indians should join the Mexicans or should harass the settlements in the rear of Taylor's army, they could bring on a serious situation; hence it was necessary to parley with the Red Brother and keep him quiet during the war. This was the plan which the Consultation had adopted in 1835, when it sent emissaries among the Indians, and made them many promises which were never fulfilled. And now when it was necessary to send the armies into Mexico, numerous councils were held among the Indians and treaties negotiated, and these conversations were continued over a long period of time, so as to keep the savage diverted, and to use a slang expression, "string him along."

As early as 1846 a Federal Indian agent had rounded up forty chiefs from this frontier, and taken them on a trip to Washington to visit President Polk, the Great Father. It was the plan of the agent to keep the chiefs traveling over the country until the war was over, and, by means of blandishments and liberal distribution of presents, the Indians were kept quiet until the close of the war.

Congress appropriated $10,000 for the Comanches and Kiowas and other prairie tribes, which was largely used during this period. Frequently this money was spent for the ransom of captives which the Indians had spirited away from the settlements and held for barter.

But when the war was over and the task of protecting the long frontier from the mouth of the Rio Grande to the remote northwest fell to the general government, there was a marked failure to meet public expectations. Almost every Governor of Texas before the Civil war complained to the Federal Government about the inefficiency of frontier protection. A Texas paper in 1849 said: "The idea of repelling mounted Indians, the most expert horsemen in the world, with a force of foot soldiers, is ridiculous."

It was charged in the House of Representatives in 1853 that the soldiers in Texas would pursue flying Comanches in wagons drawn by mules.

After 1849 the War Department increased the number of companies on the Texas frontier service from twenty-eight to forty-two, which brought the number of troops up to more than eighteen hundred, and in 1851 this force was raised to forty-eight companies, or about twenty-four hundred men. In 1853 the entire army of the United States did not exceed approximately 14,000 men, and nearly one-third of it was in service in Texas.

Bell, the third Governor of Texas, in 1852 organized three companies of rangers for service on the Rio Grande, and the Federal service was continuously supplemented by State rangers from that time until the Civil war.

Under the treaty of Guadalupe-Hidalgo, the Washington Government bound itself to protect the Mexican frontier from incursions by Indians, and consequently it had the multiplied responsibility not only of protecting the Texas frontiers, but the Mexican borders as well.

At the time of the annexation of Texas there were sixty-three military posts in the United States. In 1851 there were 109 posts, forty-six of which were in the territory acquired from Mexico, and nineteen of these in Texas. At this time there was a line of posts extending from Fort Duncan, on the Rio Grande, to Fort Marvin Scott, at Fredericksburg, Fort Croghan in Burnet County, Fort Gates in Coryell County, Fort Graham in Hill County on the Brazos, and Fort Worth in Tarrant County. This line well marked the extreme frontier, and was the imaginary line between the white man and the Indian country.

But this phantom line was soon moved westward, and before 1853 Forts Marvin Scott, Croghan, Gates and Worth had been abandoned and a new line established, and the outposts were Forts Stockton, Mason, McKavett, in Menard County; Chadbourne, now in Coke County; Phantom Hill, and Belknap, near where Graham now stands, in Young County.

During the years 1849 to 1861 many of the men who became famous in the war between the States were in Texas service. R. B. Marcy spent much of nearly twenty years here. Robert E. Lee, Kirby Smith, John B. Hood, Earl VanDorn, W. T. Hardee, George H. Thomas, George Stoneham, W. M. Graham, S. D. Sturgis, and numerous others were on the frontier rolls of the 50's.

Though the Federal forces employed on the frontier during this period were a large part of the entire standing army, the protection was wholly inadequate.

General Houston, then in the United States Senate, was a consistent critic of the Federal Indian policy, and he stated in a lecture delivered in Hartford, Connecticut, in 1852, that the National Government was then spending $6,000,000 annually to preserve peace on the frontiers of Texas and New Mexico, and that most of this was useless; that he could guarantee to keep the peace through this whole line for $100,000 a year.

The laws of Texas did not recognize the Indian's rights to the soil, though many of these tribes had occupied regional locations for centuries. After annexation the influx of immigration carried a constant tide of new homesteaders farther and farther west into the Indian country, and surveyors were constantly penetrating the hunting grounds and the State granting lands which the Indians had long claimed and looked upon as their own. The Indians were jealous over these intrusions, and, while they agreed to the location of trading posts among them, insisted that they did not relinquish their claim to the territory occupied by the traders.

Wood, the second Governor of Texas, began to complain to the Federal Government that the Indians should be removed. He said that Texas had retained all of her lands, and that they were needed for the purpose of sale and the payment of the debts of the Republic; that they could not be sold as long as the Indians infested the country, and that these Indians should be removed, since they constituted an incumbrance on the land. In fact, nothing short of their removal or extermination was ever satisfactory to the people of Texas.

The *Texas State Gazette* in 1851 announced a policy:

"The Indians must be pursued, hunted, run down, and killed, driven beyond the limits of the State."

This same paper at one time published information that the Legislature of Chihuahua had authorized the employment of agents to hunt Indians, and agreed to pay a bounty for Indian scalps; that the soldiers were to receive $200 each for warriors' scalps, and $100 each for women's and children's scalps, a higher reward for pris-

[225]

oners, and they were to have all the plunder they could secure. The same report continued that Major Chevalie, in charge of a company of emigrants from Texas for California, reached Chihuahua, and was stranded without means of continuing his journey. The Major and his company entered the Mexican service, and earned enough money in head hunting to finance their trip on to California.

The policy of the Federal Government was to concentrate the Indians on reservations, support them with annuities, and try to protect them against extermination as long as they were peaceful. This policy found great criticism among the frontier folks, who, struggling hard for a livelihood, resented the bounties which the Federal Government often gave the Indians, who were always vigilant for an opportunity to commit plunder and murder.

A Texas paper, criticising this policy, said:

"The system of bribing them to lie by giving them food and presents is behind the age, and not worthy of the nation."

It was rather an axiom from the beginning that the Texas ranger was an Indian exterminator.

In order to keep down strife, Henderson, first Governor, recommended a frontier line across which the Indians should not come and beyond which the settlers should not go. But General Houston once said to Noah Smithwick that if a wall were built, dividing the Indian country from the settlements, it could not be made so high that the white man would not scale it.

Beginning about 1850, and almost continuously until the war, the Indian depredations were constant along the entire frontier, and prior to 1857 most of them occurred in that part of the country between San Antonio and Brownsville by Indians who had learned the art of dodging across the river to escape Federal trops, and back into Texas to escape Mexican soldiers.

But the situation of the savage during this period was an unhappy one. The advance of the white population had depleted supplies of game and the buffalo was becoming scarcer. General Marcy, who was on these frontiers in the 50's, made frequent comment of the half-starved condition and constantly diminishing number of these tribes. The *Texas Telegraph* in 1849 had published a report that the Tonkaways were starving and had begged for food and offered to cease depredations if they could get enough horses to eat.

The Federal Government was unable to keep Indians from further north out of Texas during this time, and there were frequent incursions of Choctaws and Chickasaws and Kickapoos from the reservations north of Red River, who would travel all the way across Texas into Mexico on their war excursions. White traders above Red River would purchase the plunder that these Indians would take on their raids, and furnish them with guns and ammunition. It was the same old story that had been told a hundred years before, when the Comanches and Apaches would plunder the Mexican border and carry away horses and captives, which were sold at trading posts on Red River and resold to white men for slavery on the plantations in Louisiana.

THE TEXAS INDIAN RESERVATIONS.

The Federal Indian commissioners in Texas repeatedly urged that the local tribes be placed on reservations. They were in constant contact with these Indians, and represented to the authorities in Washington that they desired to settle down and become farmers and herdsmen.

In 1852 the State Legislature, in response to requests from the Federal Government, approved resolutions authorizing the Governor of Texas to negotiate lands with the national authorities for Indian reservations, and Captain Marcy and Major Neighbors were sent to survey the land. Two reservations were located in Young territory, the larger one, the Brazos agency, consisting of about 36,000 acres, was on the main fork of the Brazos River about fifteen miles south from Fort Belknap. The other reservation for the Comanches was on the clear fork of the Brazos, about forty miles above, and consisted of four leagues. On the Brazos agency Neighbors settled fragments of the Caddos, Delawares and five or six other tribes. In September, 1855, he had about 800 Indians at this agency. Houses for employes were built, and the Indians were encouraged and aided in building homes and starting farms, and they made considerable progress toward permanent settlement.

Only about 400 Indians were gathered on the Comanche reservation, and it accomplished much less than the Brazos agency, although the Indian agents from time to time made encouraging reports of progress of both reservations, and other similar reservations were proposed and discussed. The Federal Government spent about $100,000 a year upon these reservations, but they were destined to failure, because of the bitter antagonism of the white people and the continued depredations of Indians upon the settlements.

The frontiersmen repeatedly declared that the reservation Indians were guilty of these depredations, but the agents almost always insisted that it was the wild tribes and not their wards who were guilty. One J. R. Baylor, who had been Indian agent and who had been dismissed for reasons which seemed entirely sufficient, and who entertained a great hostility against Major Neighbors, devoted himself almost entirely during these years to a crusade to harass Neighbors and get rid of the Indians and break up these reservations.

Matters were brought to a climax by a raid which occurred in 1858 which frontiersmen declared was done by reservation Indians, to which Neighbors replied that the offenders were Shawnees and Kickapoos not connected with the reservation. Baylor took up this quarrel and had little difficulty in inciting the entire frontier in a campaign to wipe out the reservations. In the latter days of December, 1858, a party of twenty-seven Indians, consisting of eight men, eight women and eleven children, were camped on Keechie Creek near the lower agency. They had been hunting, and had not molested the white people, some of whom had visited them. A party of armed citizens stole up on their camp early in the morning while they slept and killed four men and three women and wounded nearly all of the others. One Peter Garland of Eastland County, and John R. Baylor and others whose names were well known, were the perpetrators of this outrage. Governor Runnels in a mild way warned the people to beware of such crimes against the Indians, but no criminal proceedings were begun against any of the persons implicated in the Keechie murders.

Baylor and his confederates continued their agitations and meetings were held in some of the frontier counties in which it was declared that they were doing for themselves what the Federal Government had failed and refused to do.

The controversy continued, and in June, 1859, Governor Runnels appointed a commission composed of George B. Erath, Richard Coke, J. M. Smith, J. M. Steiner and John Henry Brown to make an investigation. They reported no testimony incriminating the Indians

QUANAH PARKER

When the Comanches raided on Navasota Creek in 1836, they killed and captured most of the Parker family. Little Cyntha Ann, who grew to womanhood among them, became the squaw of Chief Nocona. Quanah, her son, took his mother's name, and was the last great chief of the Comanches. His mother was "rescued," and returned to her people, where she died with a broken heart pining for her savage children. Years later Quanah removed her remains from Texas, and is buried beside her at Muskogee.

of either reservation prior to the fall of 1856, but since that time they believed that both the agency and reservation Indians had been guilty of horse stealing and possibly had committed some murders; that while the majority of the Indians were faithful to the whites, there were some shrewd fellows among them who took advantage of the confidence placed in them and would steal away from the reservations; *that vicious whites had led the Indians astray.*

The situation became so tense that the Indian agents reported to the Federal Government that the further maintenance of the reservations in Texas was impossible, and Governor Runnels requested that they be removed. The Federal authorities hoped to leave them there until late in the fall, when their crops were harvested, but the pressure was so great that Neighbors reported that they had better move at once, and the exodus to the north of Red River started in June.

Volunteer troops were organized to attack the Indians if they were not removed at once, and when Neighbors took them north it was necessary to have the protection of Federal troops to prevent their destruction by angry citizens who followed the retreat.

Major Neighbors, who was a brave and efficient officer, sympathized with the Indians, and was bold in his criticisms of the attacks upon them. He returned to Fort Belknap in February, and was assassinated. In an official report to the Secretary of the Interior, following his death, Major Greenwood wrote that Neighbors was murdered by some of those whose vengeful animosity had been incurred by his zealous effort to protect the Indians and their property from wrong.

Governor Runnels was out of sympathy, as he should have been, with the agitators who brought on the Keechie murders, though he was careful not to express himself with any vigor against them. His failure to espouse the campaign of extermination, coupled with the terrible sufferings which the frontier people sustained at the hands of marauding tribes, brought down upon him the wrath of all West Texas, and this was made an issue against him in his campaign of 1859 and contributed powerfully toward his defeat.

The Federal Government recognized the inefficiency of its frontier protection during the 50's, and in 1855 Congress voted $2,500,000 to reimburse the State Government for the expenses it had incurred in ranger service during the preceding ten years.

Conditions on the frontier at the time of secession were very desperate, and the conflict for supremacy was waged for nearly twenty years longer.

One of the darkest, bloodiest chapters in the annals of the human race is the story of the white man's treatment of the Indian in America.

It began with great Columbus, who, as Governor of Hayti, started a course of cruelty to the simple natives, who in twenty years were reduced from 1,000,000 to 14,000.

We are accustomed to speak with horror of Spanish atrocities against the natives, but a close scrutiny of the conduct of our own forefathers discloses only a shade of difference. The Spaniards would enslave the Indians and waste them with drudgery and disease. The English colonists wanted their lands and found that the only way to get them and safely hold them was to exterminate the rightful owners.

One shudders to think that the great and wise generation of men who founded the colonies in Texas and wrought its independence and conserved the Republic could have been guilty of repudiating the Cherokee treaty.

It is a forbidding aspect of human progress that the civilizations of the world have been builded over the blood and ashes of weak subject races. When the white man first came to these shores, he was hailed as a superior being, and the simple native was ready to accord him the attributes of diety. But everywhere this adulation was met with ugly excesses which only a superior intellect could invent. From the time the white man came the Indian was doomed. Was it part of the Divine plan, or shall our stalwart fathers be called to answer at some far judgment day for their cruel aggressions?

Is the present reign of lawlessness which holds this country in its awful grip the outgrowth of a policy under which our fathers drove away the rightful owners of the soil and built our homes in their hunting grounds?

[231]

THE LAST INDIAN FRONTIER.

We are now to see the curtain fall on a bloody struggle of three centuries, to read the last chapter of the red man's fight for the hunting grounds of his fathers in Texas.

> "Moving westward, ever westward,
> So the red men drove their ponies
> With the tent poles trailing after
> Out along the path to sunset.
> While along the river valleys
> Came the white man close behind them,
> Men of many states and races,
> Bringing wives and children with them.
> Followed up the wooded valleys,
> Spread across the rolling prairies,
> Raising homes and reaping harvests,
> Making homes and building cities,
> Full of riches and of trouble."

In the seventies the Comanche was yet the most formidable of the tribes of our Northwestern frontier and was not essentially different from his ancestor who ruled these regions since the days of Spanish supremacy. They had been thinned by war and disease, and in the seventies buffalo ranges were giving out, and they often suffered from want. General Marcy, who was on the frontier at intervals for many years, said of them:

"Probably no people of the face of the earth are more ambitious of martial fame than the plains Indian. The attainment of such a reputation is the paramount and absorbing topic of their lives. A young man is never worthy to sit in council until he has met an enemy in battle and shows scalps in his belt."

One of the chief elements in the education of the young brave was the art of horse stealing and depredations into the settlements for horses and scalps and captives to be held for ransom. This was as much a part of the Indian's purpose in life as the chase of the buffalo. During the war the Confederate Government tried to keep up a line of defense to take the place of the Federal forces which had been maintained since the Mexican war, but pressure elsewhere had taken most of these men to other battlefields, and when the Confederacy collapsed the people were unable to defend themselves from Indian attacks, and depredations became more numerous and of greater magnitude. Throughout 1865 and 1866, the whole frontier from north to south was in constant terror, and became almost depopulated. Both Governor Hamilton and Governor Throckmorton were besieged with petitions for troops, but while Sheridan was the military overlord in Texas he refused these troops on the ground that they were needed in interior garrisons for the protection of the negroes.

In 1867, after the doughty Sheridan had scared the French out of Mexico and ousted Throckmorton from the governorship, he was sent to the Missouri-Kansas frontier, for at that time the outposts of the Federal Government reached all the way from Brownsville to Canada. His new command included the Indian Territory, and he moved among the many tribes north of the Red River who were repeatedly making incursions over our border and carrying their depredations all the way into Mexico. He reported that the Indians of the central plains were amply fed by buffalo which were yet plentiful there. He estimated that there was on these upper ranges yet six million bison to feed no more than six thousand warriors, and these well-fed Indians had so many horses that each brave could boast of twenty mounts.

During 1868 he had much war with these opulent tribes, and punished them severely, and in December was in the Wichita Mountains, where he located a permanent military camp which, in honor of General Sill, an old classmate, he named Fort Sill. He made the Comanches and Kiowas and Apaches locate in this region, and planned to keep them under surveillance and military control. The Federal Government established an agency here, and these Indians were fed, furnished arms, and being well mounted, were able to steal away for their raids into Texas, and most of the depredations committed on the Northwestern frontier during the next five or six years were done by these wards of the Government.

During this time the Federal Government had re-established its line of forts from the mouth of the Rio Grande to Fort Clark, a distance of four hundred and forty-five miles, in which space Forts Brown, Ringgold Barracks, McIntosh, Duncan, and Clark were maintained, each with a small garrison. In addition to this, a line of posts was established from Fort Clark acros the plains country to Fort Sill, including Fort McCavett, Fort Concho, Fort Griffin and Fort Richardson, a distance of five hundred and fifty-five miles, and this line of outposts was the frontier of the 70's. There was a western line of outposts along the mail route to El Paso, a distance of four hundred and ninety miles.

At that time many of the revolting tribes had established themselves permanently in Northern Mexico, and were on more or less friendly terms with their Mexican neighbors. From this vantage point, they made continual depredations across the river into Texas. A lieutenant who was stationed at Fort Clark described their incursions:

"They cross the Rio Grande in parties of no more than thirty or forty. They invariably come on foot, and when they reach this side they hide during the daytime or stay on the top of the highest mountain peaks, and when the moon is nearly or quite full, they come down. I have known them to gather two hundred horses in a single night. Then they light out, driving day and night across the river. They have no saddles, but will kill cattle and take a piece of rawhide and put a string of it over the head of a horse, pass a piece of wood through the horse's mouth for a bit, using a strip of rawhide for a bridle rein. Mounted in this way, I have known them to travel as far as eighty miles in a day and night."

The treaty under which the Indians were located on reservations across the Red River provided for the cessation of hostilities on the settlements of Texas, and, as an inducement to these marauders to cease their depredations, the Government promised to appropriate seventy-five thousand dollars annually for a period of thirty years "for the judicious purchase of such articles as may seem proper to the condition and necessities of the Indians." But the Indians never kept this treaty any part of the time.

The agent of the Wichita reservation reported in 1869 that the Comanches were depredating in Texas, and that the excuse they gave for violating their treaty was that they had never ceded away Texas, and that it was their original home. This agent stated that the Comanches had gone into Texas on no less than forty raids since they had made their treaty, and they had killed forty or fifty people, captured as many women and children, and stolen thousands of horses. He further called attention to the fact that at the very time he was writing several war parties were ravaging down in Texas.

Although on the surface the Federal Government seems to have been very liberal with these Indians, yet they had their grievances. It was published in a Texas paper as early as October, 1867, that one D. A. Butterfield, at the Indian agency, was selling the Apaches coats which cost him one dollar for eleven dollars; blankets for which he gave thirteen dollars for twenty-three dollars, and it was also published that Butterfield had made an agreement with the Kiowas to rob his train in order that he might put in a claim against the Government for losses, and that the agreement was carried out. At another time it was reported that dishonest traders were selling Indians blankets worth four dollars for twenty-two dollars.

Not only did the traders thus impose on the Indians, but they deliberately encouraged them to raid on the frontier, in order that they might sell them guns and ammunition and buy from them their stolen animals. One settler, writing from Fort Griffin in 1859, stated that the Indians were in an organization with thieves whose sole object was to make money by the traffic in stolen animals; that certain white persons would always arrive at the trading posts just in time to meet the Indians after their return from incursions into Texas with stolen horses and other plunder.

Major-General Hazen, who was stationed in this region during this time, reported to the Federal Government that the purchase of captives and plunder had been the principal incentive to the many crimes committed by the Indians, and Sheridan, who was in command here in 1867, observed that "the whole Indian management is a notorious fraud."

When these disgraceful conditions were brought to the attention of General Sheridan, he immediately gave orders to circumscribe the activities of the traders, and to forbid them to sell arms and ammunition to the savages. The sale to them of firearms had been excused on the ground that it was necessary for them to have guns for their buffalo hunts, although it was well known that the Comanche preferred to hunt buffalo with bow and arrow. Under these conditions, the Indians became bolder in carrying out their raids, and began to show an insolent attitude toward the military authorities. They would raid during the summer, and when winter came, would retreat

GENERAL WILLIAM TECUMSEH SHERMAN

The Commander in Chief of the United States Army visited the Texas frontier in 1871, and barely missed Satanta and his warriors. He and Marcy had ridden by the site of the Salt Creek massacre only an hour or so before the Indians attacked Warren's teamsters. When Gov. Davis paroled Satanta, General Sherman was indignant, and wrote: "I know Satanta will have his revenge, and if he takes scalps I hope he gets yours."

to their homes and glory in the scalps taken and the horrible debasement of the unfortunate women whom they held as prisoners.

The agent of the Wichita reservation in 1869 wrote:

"But few man know what these poor unfortunate people have suffered from the Indians, that we are feeding and clothing, during the last ten years, and are suffering now."

THE VISIT OF GENERAL TECUMSEH SHERMAN.

The lamentations of the border people were at last heard in Washington, and in April, 1871, General Sherman came to San Antonio, and on May 2nd, accompanied by General Marcy, left with an escort of seventeen men, going by way of the German village of Boerne, which contained a dozen houses. Here a discharged soldier kept a school, and the schoolmaster went constantly armed to protect himself against Indians. On May 4th they passed Fredericksburg, a German village of one thousand people. The next day they met a detachment of negro infantry who were on scout duty. Two days later they halted at Menardville and visited the ruins of the San Saba missions destroyed by the Comanches in March, 1758. Ten miles further on they met some citizens who reported an Indian raid that day, and in the evening they camped at Fort McKavett on the San Saba. Passing on by Kickapoo Springs, Fort Concho and Phantom Hill, they reached Fort Belknap on May 15th.

General Marcy's journal relates:

"We crossed immense herds of cattle today, which are allowed to run wild upon the prairies, and they multiply very rapidly. The only attention the owners give them is to brand the calves and occasionally go out to see where they range. The remains of several ranches were observed, the occupants of which have either been killed or driven off to the more dense settlements, by the Indians. Indeed, this rich and beautiful section does not contain today (May 17, 1871), as many white people as it did when I visited here years ago, and if the Indian marauders are not punished, the whole country seems to be in a fair way of being totally depopulated.

"This morning five teamsters who, with seven others, had been with a mule wagon train en route to Fort Griffin (Capt. Henry Warren's) with corn for the post, were attacked on the open prairie, about ten miles east of Salt Creek, by 100 Indians, and seven of the teamsters were killed and one wounded. General Sherman immediately ordered Colonal McKenzie to take a force of 100 cavalry, with thirty days' rations on pack mules, and pursue and chastise the marauders."

The very spot on which these men were so brutally murdered was passed over the previous day by General Sherman, General Marcy and party, and had Satanta, Big Tree, and their force attacked the General of the army, he, and those who accompanied him, or some of them, at least, might have meet the same fate as the teamsters. The route over which they had ridden from San Antonio had been traversed by Spanish troopers a hundred and twenty years before, and in 1779 DeMezieres, Indian agent and diplomat of the Spanish Government, had camped on the San Gabriel, where he wrote a letter to de Croix, the Commandant of the Eastern Internal Provinces.

The grandeur of early autumn filled the land and fired the imagination of this distinguished son-in-law of St. Denis, as he wrote:

"Few rivers can compare with the San Xavier. Obedient, its waters could irrigate the surrounding plain. Then industrious hands would bring the grain after having increased its yield. Incredible herds of cattle and horses will graze on its banks, and for variety, there will be the buffalo. There are thyme, lavender, sage, and other aromatic plants for sheep and goats. Fragrant flowers, bright adornment of the fields, will delight the bee. Hogs will fatten on the acorn, oil will be obtained from nuts. The woods and quarries will yield for building homes which will withstand the attacks of time, and be enjoyed by the grandchildren of the builders. I am unable to refrain from rapture and ecstacy."

And now, after a hundred years, his ecstatic vision was about to be realized, but

> "Not by Mexicans and Spaniards,
> Indolent and proud hidalgos
> Dwelling in their haciendas,
> While the fickle revolutions
> Change the rulers, not the people."

We are the children and grandchildren of DeMeziere's autumn vision.

On the 19th Sherman remained at Fort Richardson, and received a delegation of citizens from Jack and Parker counties who revealed to him the real conditions in Texas, and convinced him of the folly of the policy then being adopted by the military. They informed him that unless some drastic step was taken at once, the whole of the western part of the State would be depopulated. General Sherman listened attentively and grasped the entire situation. He keenly felt the humiliation of the Indian policy of the United States, acknowledged its injustice, and promised to do all in his power to remedy the conditions of affairs then existing. The deputation requested authority to go to Fort Sill to recover stock that had been stolen from them by the Indians, and General Sherman invited them to go with him the following day and identify their animals.

During the day Colonel McKenzie reported the information concerning the murder of the teamsters in Capt. Henry Warren's train was correct—that their bodies were found much mutilated, and one of the Elliott brothers "burned to a cinder." He was chained between the wheels of a wagon and a fire built under him.

On the following day Sherman left Fort Richardson and arrived at Fort Sill on the 23rd. Immediately upon his arrival he asked Tatum, the Indian agent, if he knew of any Indians having recently left the reservation, at the time telling Tatum of the Salt Creek massacre. Tatum replied that he did not know of any Indians having left the reservation, but that he would make inquiry concerning the matter. A few hours later, the chiefs Satanta, Satank, Big Tree and Eagle Heart rode to Tatum's office and he interrogated them about the raid. Satanta immediately admitted that he had led the raid into Texas, and boasted of the killing of the teamsters and the carrying away of the mules and other property. He said that he led the raid in person, and that any other chief claiming the credit for it was a liar. He gave as a reason for leading his braves into Texas that a large amount of their annuity goods had been stolen; that arms and ammunition had been refused them; that the white people were preparing to build a railway through the country, which would not be allowed. Turning to the other three chiefs standing silently by Satanta had them corroborate what he had said. Tatum immediately related this conversation to General Sherman, who asked that the Indian chiefs be sent to him.

When they arrived, Sherman questioned them concerning the raid into Texas. As in his conversation with Tatum, Satanta readily admitted that he had led the raid, and that he had blown the bugle ordering the attack. General Sherman then pointed out to him that such a raid by a party of one hundred and fifty Indians against the twelve teamsters who did not even know how to fight was a very cowardly thing to do, and that if the Indians wanted to fight his soldiers stood ready to accommodate them. He told Satanta that on account of this breach of faith on his part he and the other three chiefs associated with him in the raid were to be placed under arrest and sent back to Texas to be tried for murder. Satanta then sought to deny what he had just said concerning his part in the raid; he said that, although he was in the party that went into Texas, he had taken no part in the fight, and had gone alone to look after the wounded in another party of braves that had gone to Texas and come in contact with a band of settlers.

While the conversation was in progress, Lone Wolf, one of the Kiowa chiefs, rode up, dismounted and approached the house in which General Sherman was talking to the chiefs. He defiantly took a blanket from his shoulder and tied it about his waist, then handed a bow and quiver of arrows to one of his warriors and a gun to another. He seated himself, cocked his gun, and laid it across his lap. The detachment of soldiers standing by immediately leveled their rifles on the chiefs, and for a moment trouble seemed imminent.

Eagle Heart managed to slip away, but Satanta, Satank and Big Tree were arrested. General Sherman directed McKenzie to take them to Jacksboro, and turn them over to civil authorities there. On June 8th, McKenzie started, carrying his manacled prisoners in wagons.

Satank bitterly complained that he was a chief, and not a dog to be treated in this manner, and that he could never live over this indignity. Just before they started he called a Caddo Indian boy to his side, and said:

"I wish to send a message by you to my people. Tell them that I am dead on the side of the road; that I died the first day out, and that my bones will be lying on the side of the road. I wish my people to gather them up and take them home."

As they proceeded, Satank began a loud harangue to the other prisoners in the wagon, telling them he was a chief and a warrior, too old to be treated in this way, then, pointing to a tree where the road descended to cross a small stream about a mile away, he said:

"I shall never go beyond that tree."

Then, lifting his voice, he sang the death song:

"Oh, Sun, you remain forever, but we Kaitsenko must die.

Oh, Earth, you remain forever, but we Kaitsenko must die."

Having finished his song, he suddenly wrenched the handcuffs from his wrists, leaped on one of the guards in the wagon with him, and began to slash at him with a knife which he had managed to conceal under his blanket. The soldier leaped from the wagon, leaving his gun behind him. Satank seized the rifle and sought to load it, but was shot and killed by another member of the guard. They threw his body by the roadside, and members of his tribe came and found it, as he had told the Caddo boy.

Satank had been a chief of the Kiowas for more than twenty years, and had come in contact with Federal troops all along the border so often that he was well known to them, and had become a national character. On one hard season he decided to make friendly overtures to the supply trains along the Santa Fe Trail, in the hope of being fed, and procured a scalawag bootlegger named Peacock to write him a letter which he could show the commandants of these trains and which would certify him as the friend of the white man. So Peacock wrote:

"The bearer of this is Satank. He is the biggest liar, beggar and thief on the plains; what he can't beg of you he will steal; kick him out, for he is a lazy good for nothing Indian."

Armed with this certificate, which he could not read, he planned an easy season in which he could eat off the supply trains. He duly presented it to a passing caravan, and was severely beaten with an ox whip. After several similar experiences, it dawned on him that

[241]

there was something wrong with his certificate of character, and he procured a white trader to read it to him. When he learned its real import, he gathered a bunch of braves and visited Peacock's place, killing and scalping him, and reducing his house to ashes.

After Satank's death the slow procession moved on across the one hundred and twenty miles to Jacksboro, and its advent at Fort Richardson has been described by Lieutenant Carter:

"It was a bright day in June when he arrived with the prisoners, closely guarded by the bronzed, weather-beaten fourth cavalry. As the column halted every eye was on Satanta. He was over six feet and mounted on a small pony seemed taller. He was stark naked but for a breech clout and beaded moccasins. His coarse black hair powdered with dust hung tangled about his neck except a single scalp lock with an eagle feather to adorn it. The muscles stood out on his giant frame like knots, and his form was proud and erect in the saddle, while his motionless face and body gave him the appearance of a bronzed statue. Nothing but his intensely black glittering eyes betokened any life in his carved figure. Every feature of his face spoke disdain for the curious crowd that gathered about him. His feet were lashed with a rawhide lariat under the pony's belly, and his hands were tied. Disarmed and helpless, he was a picture of fallen savage greatness."

THE TRIAL AT JACKSBORO.

A grand jury was convened, and Satanta and Big Tree were indicted for murder. The trial in July, 1871, was one of the most interesting and spectacular that has ever occurred in the annals of Texas, and may well be ranked among the great trials in history, and its result had a far-reaching effect, as we shall see.

The presiding judge, Charles Soward, was a man under forty, and a lawyer of conspicuous ability. Samuel W. T. Lanham, the District Attorney, was a young and forceful character, who was then at the beginning of a long and useful career in Texas. The court appointed Thomas Ball and Joe Woolfork of the Weatherford bar to represent the defendants.

Thomas Williams, the foreman of the jury that was impaneled, was a frontier citizen and a brother of the Governor of Indiana.

The principal witnesses against the defendants were General McKenzie, Tatum, the Indian agent who had heard their statements at Fort Sill, and Brezeal, the teamster who had escaped from the Salt Creek massacre.

There was a vast concourse of frontier folk gathered to witness the trial. The District Attorney thus described the audience:

"This vast collection of our border people, this sea of faces, including distinguished gentlemen, civic and military, who have come hither to witness the triumph of law and justice over barbarism;

SAMUEL W. T. LANHAM OF WEATHERFORD, TWENTY-SECOND GOVERNOR
1902-04

Who prosecuted the Indian chiefs at Jacksboro thirty years before.

[243]

the matron and the maiden, the gray haired sire, and the immature lad who have been attracted to this tribunal by this unusual case, all conspire to surround it with thrilling and extraordinary interest."

Lieutenant Carter gives some touches of local color to the scene:

"Under strong guard, accompanied by his counsel and an interpreter, the chief, clanking his chain, walked to the little log courthouse on the public square. The jury had been impaneled and the District Attorney bustled and flourished around. The whole country armed to the teeth crowded the courthouse, and stood outside, listening through the open windows. The chief's attorneys made a plea for him, and referred to the wrongs the red man had suffered. How he had been cheated and despoiled of his lands and driven westward until it seemed there was no limit to the greed of the white man. They excused his crime as just retaliation for centuries of wrong. The jurors sat on log benches, each in his shirt sleeves and with shooting irons strapped to his hip."

Carter says that "the District Attorney was really quite an able little fellow, and grew eloquent in painting the horrors of the Salt Creek murder."

A fragment of District Attorney Lanham's address has been preserved:

"Satanta, the veteran council chief of the Kiowas—the orator— the diplomat—the counselor of his tribe—the pulse of his race; Big Tree, the young war chief, who leads in the thickest of the fight, and follows no one in the chase—the mighty warrior athlete, with the speed of the deer and the eye of the eagle, are before this bar in the charge of the law! So they would be described by Indian admirers who live in more secured and favored lands, remote from the frontier—where 'distance lends enchantment' to the imagination —where the story of Pocohontas and the speech of Logan, the Mingo, are read, and the dread sound of the warwhoop is not heard. We who see them today, disrobed of all their fancied graces, exposed in the light of reality, behold them through far different lenses! We recognize in Satanta the arch fiend of treachery and blood, the sinning Cataline—the promoter of strife—the breaker of treaties signed by his own hand—the inciter of his fellows to rapine and murder—the artful dealer in bravado while in the pow-wow, and the most abject coward in the field, as well as the most canting and double-tongued hypocrite where detected and overcome! In Big Tree, we perceive the tiger-demon who tasted blood and loved it as his own food—who stops at no crime how black soever—who is swift at every species of ferocity and pities not at any sight of agony or death—he can scalp, burn, torture, mangle and deface his victims, with all the superlatives of cruelty, and have no feeling of sympathy or remorse. They are both hideous and loathsome in appearance, and we look in vain to see in them anything to be admired or even endured. Still, these rough 'sons of the wood' have been commiserated; the measures of the poet and the pen of romance have been invoked to grace the 'melancholy history' of the red man. Powerful legislative influences have been brought to bear to procure for them annuities, nourish them, feed and clothe them; from their strongholds of protection they have come down upon us 'like wolves on the fold'; treaties have been solemnly made with them wherein they have been considered with all the formalities of *quasi* nationalities; immense financial 'rings' have had their origin in, and draw their vitality from, the 'Indian question'; unblushing corruption has stalked abroad, created and kept alive through

"'. . . the poor Indian, whose untutored mind,
    Sees God in clouds, or hears him in the wind.'

"Mistaken sympathy of these vile creatures has kindled the flames around the cabin of the pioneer and despoiled him of his hard earnings, murdered and scalped our people, and carried off our women into captivity worse than death. For many years, predatory and numerous bands of these 'pets of the Government' have waged the most relentless and heartrending warfare upon our frontier, stealing our property and killing our citizens. We have cried aloud for help; as segments of the grand aggregate of the country we have begged for relief; deaf ears have been turned to our cries, and the story of our wrongs has been discredited. Had it not been for General W. T. Sherman and his most opportune journey through this section—his personal observation of the debris of this scene of

[245]

slaughter, the ensanguined corpses of the murdered teamsters, and the entire evidence of this dire tragedy, it may well be doubted whether these brutes in human shape would ever have been brought to trial; for it is a fact, well known in Texas, that stolen property has been traced to the very doors of the reservation and there identified by our people, to no purpose. We are greatly indebted to the military arm of the government for kindly offices and coöperation in procuring the arrest and transference of the defendants. If the entire management of the Indian question were submitted to that gallant and distinguished officer (General McKenzie) who graces this occasion with his dignified presence, our frontier would soon enjoy immunity from these marauders."

Satanta (White Bear) had a long record, and, like Satank, had made a vicious reputation along the Santa Fe Trail and wherever he had come in contact with our soldiers and traders. He prided himself on his oratory, and was known as the orator of the plains. In 1866 General Hancock gave him a Major-General's uniform, and from some source he had gotten an ambulance, to which he had attached a fine team of stolen mules, and when not on the war path he drove over the plains in state. When President Johnson's Indian commission was in the West in 1867 it held long conferences with the various tribes, and in one of these sessions at Fort Dodge Satanta was the spokesman. He declared he had no desire to kill the white settlers, but that his people had great grievances; that the white hunters were wantonly killing their buffalo, whose carcases were left to rot, while the Indian killed only to eat. That they were burning the grass so that the Indians' horses and buffalo would starve. That they were destroying all timber along the streams, while the Indian was careful to preserve it. Holding up a green switch, he said dramatically:

"I picked this up on the trail the other day, and it made my heart bleed to think that this little branch, torn and thrown away, would have made a tree that would have sheltered our children and grandchildren."

These lofty sentiments were duly recorded and much applauded. After the day's session was over, the old rogue held a pow-wow with some congenial spirits down at the settlers' store, where he was overheard to say:

"Now, didn't I give it to these white men who came from the Great Father? I made tears in their eyes. The switch I saw on the trail made me glad. I knew some tenderfoot had dropped it, for a plainsman would use a quirt. So I said to my warriors, 'Come on, we'll get him'."

But he was now to try his oratory in dead earnest, where his life was at stake. One would hope that in this emergency he would have faced his accusers with heroic stoicism, and as his attorneys had done, recount the centuries of wrong heaped on his people. He could have told of the murder of the reservation Indians on the Keechie not twenty miles away by white men in 1859. But he cowed, lied and dissembled to save his life. Through an interpreter he addressed the court and jury. One of his first inquiries was to know if any word had come from the President, for he hoped to the last to be saved by executive clemency which was indeed freely extended to him, as we shall see.

"I cannot speak with these things upon my wrists (holding up his arms to show the iron bracelets). I am a squaw. Has anything been heard from the Great Father? I have never been so near the Tehannas (Texans) before. I look around me and see your braves, squaws and papooses, and I have said in my heart, if I ever get back to my people I will never make war upon you. I have always been the friend of the white man, ever since I was so high (indicating by sign the height of a boy). My tribe have taunted me and called me a squaw because I have been the friend of the Tehannas. I am suffering now for the crimes of bad Indians—of Satank and Lone Wolk and Kicking Bird and Big Bow and Fast Bear and Eagle Heart, and if you will let me go I will kill the three latter with my own hand. I did not kill the Tehannas. I came down to Pease River as a big medicine man to doctor the wounds of the braves. I am a big chief among my people, and have great influence among the warriors of my tribe—they know my voice and will hear my word. If you will let me go back to my people I will withdraw my warriors from Tehanna. I will take them all across the Red River and that shall be the line between us and the palefaces. I will wash out the spots of blood and make it a white land, and there shall be peace, and the Tehannas may plow and drive their oxen to the banks of the river—but if you kill me it will be like a spark in the prairie—make big fire—burn heap!"

This spectacular trial at which the chiefs of the late masters of the land were haled to the bar of the white man's court, and tried and condemned by his laws, was one of the most spectacular State trials in history. It may well be ranked with that of Mary, Queen of Scots, the impeachment of Warren Hastings, and the trial of Aaron Burr.

THE END OF THE INDIAN ON OUR FRONTIER.

No sooner had the sentence of death been pronounced on the prisoners than Enoch Hoag, superintendent of Indian affairs, began urging the President of the United States to intervene and save Satanta and Big Tree from the gallows, giving as his reason that if they were put to death war would undoubtedly follow, which would not only devastate Kansas, but the frontiers of Texas as well. Tatum, the agent at the Wichita reserve, being a Quaker, was opposed to the death sentence, and wrote the District Attorney, admonishing that one of the traits of the savage was to seek revenge, and that if the death sentence were carried out the Kiowa and Comanche would wage war on the Texas frontier. He urged that it would be a sterner punishment for these chiefs to imprison them for life than to have them executed. Judge Soward concurred in this view, and asked Governor Davis to commute their sentence to life imprisonment, which he did. Under guard furnished by General Reynolds, they were carried to the State penitentiary at Huntsville. Their imprisonment seemingly restrained the Indians for a time from raiding on the Texas frontier.

The following year the Cheyenne, Arappahoe, Comanche, Kiowa and Apache had become so menacing in their war operations that the Indian agents urged them to select a delegation of their chiefs to go to Washington for a conference with the President. They reluctantly consented, upon condition that their imprisoned chiefs should be allowed to meet and confer with them at some point along the way. The chiefs were taken from a convict gang near Denison, where they were working on the construction of the M. K. & T. Railway line, to St. Louis, where they were allowed to see and confer with their tribesmen, after which they were returned to the convict camp. The delegation went on their way to Washington, where they conferred with the Commissioner of Indian Affairs, who promised them that, if they would cease their warfare on the settlements, their captive chiefs should be released, and at once a crusade was begun for their pardon.

It became known that the Secretary of the Interior had committed himself to this agreement, and General Sherman, hearing of it, wrote:

"I hope that when Satanta is released, and he is actually killed at the head of a raiding party off his reservation as certain as next year comes, that you will simply decree that the Kiowas are outlawed, and their property confiscated and their valuable reservation restored to public domain. I believe Satanta has done fifty murders. Indeed, my idea is that the Indian by nature can't help it."

The proposal to release the prisoners met violent opposition in Texas, but was loudly encouraged by people in the North and East, and in 1873 a conference was held at Fort Sill between the Indian agents and Governor Davis, where the Governor promised to free the captive chiefs on condition that if they were ever caught raiding again they should be returned to the penitentiary at Huntsville. These conditions were readily agreed to by the representatives of the Government and of the Indian tribes, and in October, 1873, Satanta and Big Tree were released.

This caused a bitter storm of protest from all over Texas, not only from the frontier people, but the military authorities as well. General Sherman wrote Governor Davis:

"In making the tour of your frontier with a small escort I ran the risk of my life, and I said to the military commander what I now say to you—that I will not again voluntarily assume that risk at the interest of your frontier. I believe Satanta and Big Tree will have their revenge, if they have not already had it, and if they are to take scalps, I hope that yours is the first that will be taken."

[249]

The release of the prisoners had the very bad effect that the military authorities along the frontier prophesied. During the two years they were in confinement there was comparative peace. The year following more than 60 persons were killed, wounded and captured.

In 1873 General Reynolds, Commanding the Department of Texas, wrote:

"For several years the Comanches and Cheyenne have not ceased to raid in Texas, and so long as Satanta and Big Tree were in the State penitentiary they refrained from raids, but after their release there is but little doubt that the Kiowas have joined the Comanches, and they continue their forays of murder and plunder in Texas."

The year following General Auguar, who succeeded General Reynolds, wrote:

"These outrages were committed by Indians belonging to the Fort Sill reservation, where they are fed by the Government and officially regarded as friendly, and their pursuit and punishment within their reservations prohibited."

The increase in depredations from across Red River stirred the military authorities to a last vigorous campaign for summary punishments to the savages. A sufficient force was provided, and orders were given to hunt them out and chastise them wherever found. General McKenzie with one column was sent to scour the country along the fresh water fork of the Brazos, drawing his supplies from Fort Griffin, a distance of 120 miles. Lieutenant-Colonel Davidson, with six companies of cavalry, three companies of infantry, and forty-four Indian scouts, was sent west from Fort Sill, drawing his supplies from that post. Lieutenant-Colonel Buell, with another column of six companies of cavalry, two of infantry and an equipment of scouts, located his camp where Wanderers Creek empties into Red River, and campaigned from that point. General Nelson A. Miles, with eight companies of the Sixth Cavalry, and four companies of infantry, was sent to coöperate with the above forces, and Major Price marched from Fort Union along the Canadian River as far as Antelope Hills.

As a result of these several converging military expeditions, the Indians were severely punished. They were given no rest, day or night, summer or winter. The soldiers followed them up to their hunting grounds, and by the middle of 1874 many of the tribes surrendered to escape the vengeance of the soldiers.

Late in the year Satanta and Big Tree and several other chiefs came with a large number of their people to the Cheyenne agency at Darlington, and surrendered, stating that they were tired of war, but did not like Fort Sill. Satanta, who was known to have broken

SATANTA IN PRISON

After he was returned to the penitentiary in 1874, he saw no hope of escape. For awhile he was worked on a chain gang wihch helped to build the M. K. & T. Railway. He became sullen and broken in spirit, and would be seen standing for hours gazing through his prison bars towards the north, the hunting grounds of his people. In October, 1876, he committed suicide by throwing himself from a window.

[251]

his parole, was arrested, and in November of that year returned to the penitentiary at Huntsville, but Big Tree escaped and was never recaptured. Satanta was so depressed at being returned to prison that he made a very sullen prisoner, and in October, 1876, committed suicide by throwing himself from an upper story window.

The campaign which began in 1874 was continued without abatement until in February of the next year, when the remnant of the tribes that had not surrendered came in and submitted to authority.

The experience of the imprisonment of the chiefs in the Texas penitentiary had proven so salutary that the military authorities selected seventy-five of the ringleaders of the late disturbances and sent them to military prisons in Florida.

The arrest, conviction and imprisonment of Satanta and Big Tree, followed by the vigorous campaigns of 1874 and 1875, broke the spirit of the warring tribes and ended Indian depredations on the Texas frontier.

Here we witness the close of the conflict that raged for centuries for the mastery of Texas. It began when LaSalle's fort and followers were destroyed on Matagorda Bay in the seventeenth century, and went on and on during the days of thirty viceroys who strove with soldier and priest to extend Spanish dominion over Texas. Fifty years of border warfare had raged since Austin's colonists came.

> "Yet they never failed or faltered
> Till their toil was crowned with triumph
> And the country of the Tejas
> Was the fertile land of Texas."

Squads of surveying parties now began to cover all West and Northwest Texas, locating land grants for homesteaders and railroads. On the heels of the land locators emigrant trains moved forward and the settlements were no longer confined to the shadow of the forts.

The necessity for the garrisons was soon gone, and in 1878 the last of the outposts which had been established on this frontier at the close of the Mexican war thirty years before was abandoned.

The slavery issue was settled, the Indian question gone, and our people turned to face a new era with new problems full of infinite perplexities.

"Moving westward, ever westward,
So the red men drove their ponies
With the tent poles trailing after
Out along the path to sunset."

C. R. WHARTON.

Bay Ridge,
September 21, 1934